FLAT TAX: TOWARDS A BRITISH MODEL

By Allister Heath

CW01082625

The author

Allister Heath is Associate Editor of *The Spectator* magazine and Deputy Editor of *The Business* newspaper. He has been a regular contributor to the *Scotsman* and *Scotland on Sunday* in Edinburgh and he has also written for many other newspapers and magazines, such as *The Wall Street Journal Europe, Economic Affairs* and *The European Journal.* Heath went to school in France and holds a B.Sc. in Economics from the London School of Economics and an M.Phil. in Economics from Oxford University. He was awarded the Honourable Mention in the annual Frederic Bastiat international journalism prize in October 2005.

Acknowledgments

I would like to thank Matthew Elliott of The TaxPayers' Alliance and Sacha Kumaria of the Stockholm Network for initiating this project and David B Smith of Williams de Broe for helpful comments. But by far my greatest debt is to Neda for her loving help and for putting up with me writing this book in my spare time – of which, as she knows all too well, I have very little. Needless to say, any errors in this book are mine alone. Comments are welcome at allister_heath@yahoo.co.uk

Published by the Stockholm Network (www.stockholm-network.org) and
The TaxPayers' Alliance (www.taxpayersalliance.com)

Price: £10.00

ISBN: 0-9547663-6-9

"Thou shalt truly tithe all the increase of thy seed that the field bringeth forth year by year"
— Deuteronomy 14:22 (King James Version), endorsing a flat tax

"It should be known that at the beginning of a dynasty, taxation yields a large revenue from small assessments. At the end of the dynasty, taxation yields a small revenue from large assessments... the strongest incentive for cultural activity is to lower as much as possible the amounts of individual imposts levied upon persons capable of undertaking cultural enterprises. In this manner, such persons will be psychologically disposed to undertake them, because they can be confident of making a profit from them."
— Ibn Khaldûn, 14th century Arab philosopher, in The Muqaddimah, the most important Islamic history of the pre-modern world [1]

"An inquisition into every man's private circumstances, and an inquisition which, in order to accommodate the tax to them, watched over all the fluctuations of his fortunes, would be a source of such continual and endless vexation as no people could support... The proprietor of stock is properly a citizen of the world, and is not necessarily attached to any particular country. He would be apt to abandon the country in which he was exposed to a vexatious inquisition, in order to be assessed to a burdensome tax, and would remove his stock to some other country where he could either carry on his business, or enjoy his fortune more at his ease. By removing his stock he would put an end to all the industry which it had maintained in the country which he left. Stock cultivates land; stock employs labour. A tax which tended to drive away stock from any particular country would so far tend to dry up every source of revenue both to the sovereign and to the society. Not only the profits of stock, but the rent of land and the wages of labour would necessarily be more or less diminished by its removal."
— Adam Smith, political economist, 1776 [2]

"Nor should the argument seem strange that taxation may be so high as to defeat its object, and that, given sufficient time to gather the fruits, a reduction of taxation will run a better chance than an increase of balancing the budget."
— John Maynard Keynes, economist idolised by the political left [3]

"An economy hampered by restrictive tax rates will never produce enough revenues to balance our budget just as it will never produce enough jobs or enough profits... In short, it is a paradoxical truth that tax rates are too high today and tax revenues are too low and the soundest way to raise the revenues in the long run is to cut the rates now."
— John F. Kennedy, former Democratic President of the US [4]

"The bureaucratic maze that mankind has built itself is not gonna go away. It's just there. I guess it's like trying to put through the flat tax, which is probably my favorite one of all. Because everyone talks about it, likes the idea, but all you hear are all the reasons it won't work. But if we did pass it, all of a sudden, what do you have? You have the whole tax system run by a little old lady on a home computer, doing the work of all these thousands of bureaucrats and accountants. Passing that would be amazing, wouldn't it?"
— Clint Eastwood, Hollywood director and film star [5]

1   Ibn Khaldûn [English edition] (1969), *The Muqaddimah*, Bollingen
2   Adam Smith (1776), *An Inquiry into the Nature and Causes of the Wealth of Nations*, Edited by R.H. Campbell, A.S. Skinner and W.B. Todd, Liberty Fund, 1982
3   John Maynard Keynes (1972), *The Collected Writings of John Maynard Keynes*, Macmillan/Cambridge University Press, London
4   John F. Kennedy, Speech to Economic Club of New York, 14 December 1962.
    http://www.americanrhetoric.com/speeches/jfkeconomicclubaddress.html
5   'The age of Eastwood: Clint on fame, directing daughter Alison in Midnight 7, why Dirty Harry is History', Denis Mamill, *New York Daily News*, 19 November 1997

Contents

Foreword by Steve Forbes

This book couldn't be more timely. The flat tax is indeed an idea whose time is coming – and the global economy – including Britain's – will enormously benefit from it. Allister Heath has done a superb job in explaining the concept, dealing with the arguments routinely used to oppose this radical, pro-liberty approach to taxation and surveying countries that have adopted variations of it.

The flat tax is a powerful generator of economic growth. A single tax rate is applied to personal incomes after generous exemptions for adults and children. For businesses, the profits tax would also be very low and businesses would be allowed to expense immediately all capital investments instead of writing the assets off over several years. Under the plan I proposed for the U.S., for instance, a family of four would owe no federal income tax on their first $46,000 of income and would pay only 17% on any income above that $46,000. For a family of six, the exemption would amount to more than $65,000. There would be no tax on savings – no levies on dividends, interest and capital gains. For businesses, the profits tax would be cut from the present rate of 35% to 17% and business investments would be expensed immediately.

Hong Kong was the first to apply a variation of the flat tax nearly sixty years ago and it has worked magnificently. It played a key role in transforming Hong Kong from one of the poorest areas on earth to one of the most prosperous. In recent years ten countries – Estonia, Latvia, Lithuania, Russia, Ukraine, Slovakia, Georgia, Romania, Serbia and Iraq – have adopted a flat tax and it has worked well everywhere. As the Prime Minister of Estonia put it not so long ago, "Once you've tried it, you never want to go back".

A number of countries including Spain, Greece, Croatia and Slovenia, are considering the flat tax. Support is growing among policymakers in Germany – and as this book demonstrates, in Britain (whoever could have conceived a few years ago that the Liberal Democrats would give the idea serious consideration) – to do the same. China is also examining the issue.

A critical principle to understanding why the flat tax is so potent in fuelling economic growth is that taxes are not just a means of raising revenue for government; they are also a price and a burden. The tax you pay on income is the price you pay for working. The tax you pay on profits is the price you pay for being successful. And the tax on capital gains is the price you pay for taking risks that work out. The concept is thus very simple – when you lower the price of positive things such as productive work, risk-taking and success, you get more of them. Raise the burden and price, and you will get less of them.

What policymakers so often can't grasp is that reducing tax rates does not reduce tax revenues. Lowering rates increases incentives for people to start new businesses and to work more productively.

This is not theory. In the U.S., for example, every time the federal income tax rates have been cut, the American economy has gotten stronger and federal tax receipts have ended up increasing, not decreasing. Employment has gone up.

In the 1960s then-President John Kennedy proposed a 23% reduction across the board in American income tax rates. Critics cried that this would unacceptably reduce Washington's tax receipts. The cuts were eventually enacted and the American economy boomed – and Washington's tax take went up. We saw a similar phenomenon in the 1980s when Ronald Reagan's radical income tax rate reductions were fully enacted. During the 1980s, federal tax receipts just about doubled even though the top tax rate dropped from 70% to 28%.

Other countries have had similar experiences. Russia enacted a flat tax in 2001 to a low level of 13%. Russia's income tax receipts, adjusted for inflation, more than doubled within four years.

Nobel Prize-winning economist Edward Prescott has shown the effect that high taxes have on a country's workers. Prescott examined the question: Why do Americans work so much more than western Europeans?

His findings reveal that Americans work 50 % more than their counterparts in France, Germany, and Italy. Very high tax rates in those countries persuade people to work less. These findings also hold true for non-Western cultures like Japan.

Prescott demonstrated that, historically, when the French and others were taxed similarly to Americans, they worked the same amount of time. Europeans only began to work less as their tax rates increased, creating today's huge disparity between American and European productivity.

The flat tax's simplicity also means greater compliance as the Russian experience dramatically demonstrates – Russia previously had a horrific system of unimaginable complexity that bred widespread non-compliance and rampant corruption. When the tax code is transparent and easily understandable, people have a hard time evading it. In fact, since the rate is so low most people and most businesses don't think it is worth the risk to try to avoid what they lawfully owe.

As you would expect there are variations of the flat tax. Each of the countries that have adopted it has a different rate. And some countries still have a more traditional income tax system – but with very low rates.

But the concept is the same – low taxes and simplicity are a potent mix for greater prosperity.

For example, utilising sophisticated economic modeling that takes into account the real world context of tax changes, Fiscal Associates has determined that, over the course of ten years, the flat tax would create in the U.S. $6 trillion in new assets, $892 billion in additional payroll tax receipts and lead to nearly 3.5 million new jobs that otherwise would not exist. The flat tax would cut the tax burden on all Americans.

Some opponents claim the flat tax would help only the rich. Wrong. Not only would it be a tax cut for everyone, it would also abolish all those loopholes that are seen as benefiting the rich. The flat tax would make it harder for those commanding armies of tax lawyers and lobbyists to manipulate the system. By creating more prosperity, the flat tax enables people just starting out in life a greater opportunity to get jobs and then to move on to better paying jobs.

This has certainly been the experience of those countries where the flat tax has been implemented.

No wonder the flat tax idea is rapidly spreading. Countries are increasingly recognising that if they don't adopt the flat tax, they will lose jobs and capital and ambitious entrepreneurs to growth-friendly nations. In other words, just as competition is essential for economic progress, so, too, tax competition spurs more growth and opportunity.

One sees the benefit of tax competition already on the corporate side. Austria last year slashed its corporate tax rate from 34% to 25% because neighboring central European countries had lowered rates and were attracting job creating investments. The Netherlands recently reduced rates and other European countries are following suit.

As the late, great banker Walter Wriston never tired of observing, capital – money and people – goes where it is welcome and stays where it is well treated.

The flat tax movement is being recognised by media organisations that had once been sceptical, including the Economist magazine, which devoted an April 2005 cover story to the growing worldwide support for the flat tax.

The flat tax would enormously help western Europe to come out of its economic doldrums and generate desperately needed growth. Countries such as France and Germany are plagued with high employment, which leads to destabilising social unrest. Britain needs the flat tax. Yes, the country transformed itself from Europe's sick man of the 1960s and '70s into the economic dynamo of the past two decades. But an endless array of "stealth" taxes is starting to clog Britain's economic arteries. The flat tax will clean those arteries and enable the U.K. again to grow rapidly.

Steve Forbes

Steve Forbes is President and Chief Executive Officer of Forbes and Editor-in-Chief of Forbes *magazine. In both 1996 and 2000, Mr. Forbes campaigned vigorously for the Republican nomination for the Presidency. Key to his platform were a flat tax, medical savings accounts, a new Social Security system for working Americans, parental choice of schools for their children, term limits and a strong national defense. Mr. Forbes continues to energetically promote this agenda. Mr. Forbes is the author of the recently published* Flat Tax Revolution: Using a Postcard to Abolish the IRS *(Regnery, 2005). He also wrote* A New Birth of Freedom *(Regnery, 1999), a book of bold ideas for the new millennium.*

Chapter I: Introduction

For those of us who have consistently advocated a flat tax for Britain long before it became fashionable, it is gratifying to witness the explosion of interest in the idea over the past few months. The Conservative Party, for years an ideas-free zone, and the Liberal Democrats, probably still Britain's most left-wing mainstream party, have jumped on the bandwagon and are taking the idea seriously, even though it is now clear they are not yet ready for its full radicalism. George Osborne, the Tory shadow chancellor, says he supports "flatter taxes"[6] and has set up a commission to study the idea[7]; his counterpart at the Liberal Democrats, Vince Cable, has also set up a study group to investigate options for tax reform and made some positive noises about flatter and simpler taxes, though he also rejects a full flat tax.[8]

But the real proof that the flat tax has arrived as a serious option for policy change in Britain is that over the past few months it has come under a sustained barrage of criticism from Chancellor Gordon Brown's Treasury and numerous left-wing think-tanks, economists and media commentators, who until now had dismissed the policy as too radical or mad to bother criticising. The flat tax is even being blamed for the disappointing performance of Germany's new Christian Democrat Chancellor, Angela Merkel, in the 18 September 2005 elections, even though she never actually endorsed the policy. Opponents are now wrongly but all too predictably pointing to Merkel's failure to win an outright victory to warn that any party in Britain that embraces the flat tax would suffer the same sorry fate.

Under a comprehensive flat tax, all income earned by individuals and companies, other than a tax-free personal allowance, is taxed at a single, low rate. There are no exemptions or exceptions – and no loopholes – and none of the multiple tax bands and rates invariably associated with traditional tax systems; sometimes, flat tax proposals also include aligning the rate of value added tax with that on income. In its purest, academic form, a flat tax is accompanied by other reforms, such as the abolition of the double taxation of profits, the ending of inheritance tax and other worthy changes intended to abolish the double taxation of income. Proponents of the flat tax would like taxpayers to pay their taxes using a couple of postcard-size forms, preferably via the internet: one form for personal income; the other for business income. According to Adam Smith, a country's tax system should strive to be efficient, transparent, simple and fair[9]; while no tax system is perfect, a flat tax is much closer to matching Smith's criteria than our present system.

---

6   'Achieving lower, simpler taxes', George Osborne, Social Market Foundation, 7 September 2005:
     http://www.conservatives.com/tile.do?def=news.story.page&obj_id=124663&speeches=1
7   'Conservatives to examine "flat tax" option', *Conservatives.com*, 5 September 2005
     http://www.conservatives.com/tile.do?def=news.story.page&obj_id=124614
8   'Lib Dems dismiss 'flat tax' as reform option', *ePolitix.com*, 14 September 2005
     http://www.epolitix.com/EN/News/200509/48520b79-3a2d-40bb-b2be-1812a657ee50.htm
9   Smith, op. cit.

By far the most important advantage of adopting a flat tax is the boost to economic growth it entails. By getting rid of high marginal tax rates, flat taxes make hard work more rewarding (and therefore encourage it) and increase the opportunity cost of leisure (and thus discourage it). By improving the returns to work, a flat tax can be expected to increase the supply of labour (especially of women and older men), facilitate entrepreneurship, risk-taking and the creation of small businesses, make investment more worthwhile, including spending on human capital (such as education and training), help attract foreign direct investment, overseas capital and migrants (especially skilled, high-productivity workers), and bring part of the grey economy into the official economy because tax rates are kept lower, thus reducing the incentive for avoidance or moving assets into foreign tax havens. A comprehensive flat tax system with low tax rates also has huge benefits in terms of reduced compliance costs. It would broaden the tax base by curtailing the incentive for an underground economy and thereby reduce tax evasion, avoidance and underreporting. Under a flat tax, it would also be easier and cheaper to pay taxes without having to use expensive accountants and advisers, destroying the rationale for tax planning or income shifting; the cost of collecting taxes would also be lower.

At present, many corporate and individual decisions are taken for tax reasons, disrupting the economy and ensuring that the allocation of resources is not as efficient as it could be; most of these distortions would be eliminated under a comprehensive flat tax. For individuals, there would no longer be any need for complex and bureaucratic investment vehicles such as individual savings accounts (ISAs), for example.

Sweeping away the current convoluted and damaging UK tax code and replacing it by a flat tax would also have another important effect: it would send the country a powerful signal that there is nothing morally wrong with hard work and success. Instead of being punished for earning more than average, high earners would be treated in exactly the same way as everybody else. This psychological impact would gradually contribute to a further spreading of a philosophy which elevates the desire for self-betterment and which welcomes, rather than resents, success.

The kind of flat tax envisaged by most of its proponents would also be of immediate direct and indirect benefit to the poor. It would take many out of the direct tax system altogether – more than 8m households, in the model developed in the penultimate chapter of this book (defining direct taxes here as income tax and national insurance contributions). The gains from my proposal would be concentrated on the bottom 30% of the population; the top 30% would be only marginally better off in the short-term (see Chapter 9 for the details). Fewer people would have to pay direct tax on the one hand while simultaneously collecting offsetting handouts on the other; this would make it easier and more worthwhile for the most vulnerable to extricate themselves from the welfare trap. By boosting economic growth, it would also improve employment and provide more opportunities for the poor. All of this suggests that the flat tax would do wonders for social mobility in Britain, which many believe has unfortunately ceased to improve in recent years and may even have started to decline.[10]

Under a flat tax, the economy would perform better and people would be less likely to avoid paying their taxes. Tax revenues would thus be reduced by less than expected in the short term, despite lower tax rates; in the long run tax receipts would go up, at least by the same rate as nominal economic growth and perhaps faster. Dynamic effects on growth and revenues would confound sceptics and refute claims that a flat tax would punch a massive hole in the government's finances. Remarkably, a flat tax would do what every other tax cut has accomplished in Britain since 1979 and ensure that the better-off pay a larger share of the overall tax burden, a result that the left ought to be happy with.

In an interesting development, the UK Treasury was recently forced to release some of the research it had secretly conducted into the pros and cons of a flat tax. The version published on the Treasury website was suitably censored and came out hard against the idea; however, a complete version later obtained by George Osborne revealed a much more balanced document.[11] Here is a choice quote: "The combined effect of savings in compliance and yield increases should then enable a cut in average taxes and spur further reductions in tax avoidance and evasion, shrinking the grey economy, and increasing the attractiveness of the economy to foreign investors, creating a mini-economic boom". I couldn't have put it better myself.

It would be unfair to take this paragraph as meaning that the Treasury agrees with a flat tax – it doesn't; the document goes on to raise numerous objections, almost all of them flawed. But at least (some of) its researchers are aware of (some of) the arguments, even if their bosses – who remained wedded to the idea that the better-off should be punished and the poor guided and induced to behave in ways that are supposedly good for them, thanks to a horrendously complex system of tax credits and other means-tested benefits – remain bitterly opposed to any new thinking.

This is a great pity. As an extraordinarily powerful yet remarkably simple idea, the flat tax is fast becoming the most influential new free-market policy since privatisation and the fight against inflation caught the world's imagination during the late 1970s and early 1980s. Although the idea has been around for years – one relatively modern proposal can be found in Milton Friedman's 1963 book, Capitalism and Freedom[12] – it was first mooted in its formal, modern incarnation by two brilliant American economists, Robert E Hall, a vice president of the American Economic Association, senior fellow of the Hoover Institution and professor of economics at

10 Jo Blanden, Paul Gregg and Steve Machin (2005), *Intergenerational Mobility in Europe and North America*, Centre for Economic Performance, London School of Economics - http://cep.lse.ac.uk/about/news/IntergenerationalMobility.pdf. For a critical analysis of the paper, see 'Blame poor schooling for our lack of social mobility', Allister Heath, *The Business*, 26 June 2005.
11 Flat Taxes, HM Treasury, 2005. An uncensored version of the document is obtainable at http://www.taxfoundation.org/UserFiles/Image/Blog/FLAT%20TAXES%20-%20HMT%20release2.doc; the official version can be found at http://www.hm-treasury.gov.uk/media/CFA/92/foi_flattax010805.pdf
12 Milton Friedman (1963), *Capitalism and Freedom*, University Of Chicago Press

Stanford University, and his colleague Alvin Rabushka, also a senior fellow of the Hoover Institution, in articles published in 1981[13] and then in a hugely influential book, The Flat Tax, first published in 1985 and now in its second edition.[14]

Versions of the flat tax have operated in Jersey and Guernsey since 1940 and 1960 respectively and in Hong Kong since 1947. But it was far-sighted countries in Eastern and Central Europe that were the first to throw down the flat tax gauntlet to the rest of Europe, leading by example and using their new found competitive advantage for all it is worth. By the early 1990s, an (admittedly imperfect) version of the flat tax had been adopted in Estonia, then under the leadership of a brilliant young prime minister, Mart Laar. Since then, more and more countries have jumped on to the bandwagon, adopting more or less comprehensive versions of the flat tax, and the pressure is now on for the first western European economy to join the party. Among the countries able to boast of having adopted a flat tax of one sort or another (none is fully comprehensive as described in Hall-Rabushka) are Estonia (1994, 26%), Lithuania (1994, 33%), Latvia (1995, 25%), Russia (2000, 13%), Serbia (2003, 14%), Ukraine (2004, 13%), Slovakia (2004, 19%), Georgia (2005, 12%), and Romania (2005, 16%). Since 2001, the Canadian province of Alberta has operated a 10% provincial flat tax; there is currently a debate in Utah, USA, to turn the state income tax into a flat tax, probably of 5%, albeit with a few exemptions. Utah wants to move its state income tax (but not all other taxes) to a flat tax but has faced opposition from the Mormon Church which doesn't want to lose the tax advantages for charitable donations. Illinois, Indiana, Massachusetts, Michigan and Pennsylvania have a flat state tax on personal income, ranging from 3% in Illinois to 5.3% in Massachusetts (Pennsylvania's is a pure flat tax, with no zero-bracket amount); however all these states also charge other sorts of taxes.[15]

A flat tax has a particularly poignant appeal in that it would finally consign a key plank of Marxism to the dustbin of history. In their infamous Communist Manifesto, first published in 1848, Karl Marx and Friedrich Engels, two of history's most destructive and flawed thinkers, demanded "a heavy progressive or graduated income tax".[16] This was listed as second only in importance to the communist vision after the "abolition of property in land". For the nations of Eastern and Central Europe, which had to endure the abomination of Marxist-inspired Communist regimes for many decades, the eradication of graduated rates of tax has been a great symbolic victory for freedom and democracy.

So far, Western governments have been hesitant to go the whole hog and adopt a flat tax, preferring to cut top rates instead. Increasingly worried by the threat of tax

---

13 'The Attractions of a Flat-Rate Tax System', Alvin Rabushka, The Wall Street Journal, 25 March 1981; 'A Proposal to Simplify Our Tax System', Robert E. Hall and Alvin Rabushka, The Wall Street Journal, 10 December 1981; Robert E Hall & Alvin Rabushka (1983), Low Tax, Simple Tax, Flat Tax, McGraw-Hill.
14 Robert E. Hall and Alvin Rabushka (1995), The Flat Tax (Second Edition), Stanford, CA, Hoover Institution Press:
    http://www-hoover.stanford.edu/publications/books/flattax.html
15 'Flat tax', Wikipedia
    http://en.wikipedia.org/wiki/Flat_tax
16 Karl Marx and Friedrich Engels (1848), Manifesto of the Communist Party:
    http://www.anu.edu.au/polsci/marx/classics/manifesto.html

competition, even the French are planning some income tax cuts and simplification, ahead of the 2007 presidential elections. The Paris government promised in September 2005 a major tax reform to take effect two years later, including cuts in the number of tax brackets to four from seven, the elimination of several exemptions and limitations on the combined income and wealth tax burden. The Spanish government has proposed tax cuts for those on lower-incomes and companies.

More and more top economists support a flat tax. In Italy, Renato Brunetta, chief economic adviser to Prime Minister Silvio Berlusconi, strongly favours a flat tax, as does Defence Minister Antonio Martino. Two senior economic advisers in Spain – Miguel Sebastian, Director of the Spanish Economic Office, and Manuel Díaz-Mendoza, of the Prime Minister's Economic Bureau – have also advocated a flat tax. In Australia, new Nationals federal president David Russell has mooted the idea of his party embracing a flat tax, as it did unsuccessfully in the 1980s.[17] Minor parties in Denmark and Finland are also advocating a flat tax; the main opposition party in the Czech Republic also agrees. On 28 September 2005, the Dutch Council of Economic Advisors recommended to the lower house of Parliament that it should introduce a 40% flat rate of income tax.[18] Under the Coalition Provisional Authority, L. Paul Bremer, the U.S. administrator in Baghdad, gave Iraq a 15% flat tax.[19]

But the flat tax has also suffered some important setbacks recently. Greek Finance Minister Giorgos Alogoskoufis announced in July 2005 that he hoped to introduce a flat tax of 25%; unfortunately nothing has come of this yet. Poland already has an optional flat tax of 19% for employers; while supporters of the flat tax failed to win the 25 September elections, at least their influence means that the country's taxes are set to be cut and reformed in a positive direction. In Australia, Treasurer Peter Costello commissioned research into a flat tax at 30% in the run up to the 2005 Budget in May but decided not to proceed; getting rid of the top 47% rate would supposedly have reduced tax revenues by more than A$16bn and so the policy was not adopted.[20]

The idea recently had a good airing in Germany, though Christian Democrat leader Angela Merkel's failure to win outright at the general election on 18 September 2005 means that a move is unlikely any time soon. Nevertheless, last year, Wolfgang Wiegard, head of the government's council of economic advisers, proposed a 30% flat tax; needless to say Chancellor Gerhard Schroder didn't listen. Paul Kirchof, a leading advocate of the flat tax, advised the Merkel campaign and became the far-left's hate figure, being blamed by some in the media for Merkel's failure. The truth is that Merkel never supported a real flat tax herself; in any case, it takes time and a sustained

17 'Push to revisit Joh's flat tax rate', Elizabeth Colman, *The Australian*, 20 September 2005
18 'Dutch Council of Economic Advisors Recommends Flat-Tax System to Parliament', James Auger, *Global Insight Daily Analysis*, 28 September 2005; and see also http://www.tweedekamer.nl/leden_commissies_fracties/economisch_adviseurs_rea/index.jsp
19 Dana Milbank & Walter Pincus, US Administrator Imposes Flat Tax System on Iraq, *Washington Post*, 2 November 2003, http://www.globalpolicy.org/security/issues/iraq/occupation/2003/1102tax.htm
20 Mary Swire, 'Howard Makes Light Of Australian Government's Flat Tax Study', *Tax-News.com*, 17 October 2005: http://www.tax-news.com/asp/story/story_open.asp?storyname=21456

campaign to implement radical tax reform, something which Merkel failed to do.

Even if Germany, increasingly a basket case economy held back by defective political institutions and a population that has grown too complacent for its own good, has yet to have the guts to embrace a flat tax, it is clearly an idea whose time has come in more dynamic, up-and-coming parts of the world.

In the Czech Republic, the leading opposition party has pledged to introduce a 15% flat tax if elected. Slovenia's Strategic Council for Economic Development recommended a 20% flat income tax in May 2005; there are signs that Slovenia will be the 10th Eastern European country to adopt a flat tax-type system, probably in 2007. A 10% flat tax was proposed in April 2005 by a Special Commission for Fiscal Reform in Puerto Rico[21]; and even the Chinese have considered a flat rate of 20% and appear to remain interested in the idea.

In America, the flat tax debate has been raging for years, led by free-market think-tanks such as the Cato Institute, the Heritage Foundation and Freedom Works, and several prominent Republican politicians, including Dick Armey[22] and many others.[23] A new book on the subject by publisher and former presidential candidate Steve Forbes is the latest of many offerings.[24] President Bush is committed to tax reform and has introduced several successful supply-side tax cuts since his election in 2000, despite intense opposition from the political left. Unfortunately, President Bush's complicity in and encouragement of the public spending explosion of recent years, his troubles in Iraq, dithering over Supreme Court nominations and his increasing lack of political nous and congenital inability to wage a competent public relations campaign outside of elections means that radical tax reform now seems dead on arrival in the US.[25]

Unless Gordon Brown can be persuaded of the merits of a flat tax, and fast, Britain will continue its slide down the competitiveness league tables, condemning itself to becoming an also-ran in today's increasingly tough global economy. Nowadays, the UK's competition is no longer merely to be found in Old Europe; in the era of the internet and globalisation, it is everywhere, from Shanghai to Chicago.

The purpose of this book is to add to the existing international debate on the flat tax, as well as provide UK-specific analysis and policy recommendations. Most discussions in the UK have been too limited, focusing only on cutting the top and bottom

21 'The Flat Tax may spread to the Commonwealth of Puerto Rico', Alvin Rabushka, *RussianEconomy.org*, 6 June 2005:
   http://www.russianeconomy.org/comments/060605.html
22 Dick Armey (1996), *The Flat Tax: A Citizen's Guide to the Facts on What It Will Do for You, Your Country, and Your Pocketbook*, Ballantine Books.
23 Daniel J. Mitchell (1995), *Jobs, Growth, Freedom, and Fairness: Why America Needs a Flat Tax*, Heritage Foundation, http://www.heritage.org/Research/Taxes/BG1035.cfm ; Daniel J. Mitchell (1996), *The Flat Tax: Freedom, Fairness, Jobs, and Growth*, Regnery Publishing; 'A brief guide to the flat tax', Daniel J. Mitchell, July 2005:http://www.heritage.org/Research/Taxes/bg1866.cfm. A list and explanation of the numerous proposals in the US Congress can be found in James M. Bickley (2005), *Flat Tax Proposals and Fundamental Tax Reform: An Overview*, CRS Issue Brief for Congress, Congressional Research Service, The Library of Congress, http://shelby.senate.gov/legislation/Taxes-Flat.pdf
24 Steve Forbes (2005), *Flat Tax Revolution: Using a Postcard to Abolish the IRS*, Regnery Publishing
25 The conclusions of his Tax Reform Commission – which unfortunately didn't endorse a flat tax – came too late for this book. They are available at http://www.taxreformpanel.gov

rates of income tax rather than overhauling the entire tax system, which is what the brains behind the original idea always intended. This book therefore starts by summarising and explaining the original Hall-Rabushka proposal.

Another limitation of the UK (and much of the European) debate is the absence of any references to the academic literature of the flat tax: many professional economists have invested a lot of time and effort trying to assess the consequences and impact of moving towards a Hall-Rabushka tax system and it is worth being aware of the results of their work. This book's next contribution is to provide an up-to-date review of a selection of the academic literature, both on the flat tax per se and on related areas, including the strong link between lower taxes and stronger economic growth.

The book goes on to rehearse all the arguments in favour of a flat tax, highlighting in particular some of the less obvious ones, as well as some little-known academic papers and research backing up some of the arguments. Without gaining a proper understanding of how the British tax and benefit system works (or fails to work), it is difficult to know how it should be reformed, so I also highlight some of its more disturbing aspects. Much of this material is extremely complex, especially those aspects that relate to the interaction of income tax and national insurance contributions, benefits and tax credits.

I continue by reviewing all previous British proposals endorsing a version of the flat tax, including the well-known Adam Smith Institute paper as well as lesser-known models; before presenting and analysing all the main UK research papers criticising the flat tax. As such, I believe that my book represents the only thorough overview of the UK debate. My next chapter reviews in some detail the tax systems in all those Eastern European countries with flat tax-type systems, pointing out how far they have gone and how much further they still have to go if they want to move towards a pure Hall-Rabushka flat tax.

Finally, I outline my own proposal, explaining how a first giant step towards a flat tax could be taken. This would include slashing income tax as well as cutting national insurance contributions and merging the two systems into one, with a single flat 28% rate on income from wages and salaries above £9,000 a year. Crucially, this would be only a first step and the aim would be to lower this rate over time. All loopholes would be repealed, as would be inheritance tax, capital gains tax, the tax on dividends and tax on interest. Company profits would also be subject to a single 28% rate on profits, also above a generous allowance. Tax credits would be abolished and partly replaced by traditional welfare benefits. There would be only one exception to the 28% flat tax: pensioners would enjoy a lower, 22% rate. This is because income from pensions as well as the salaries, wages and self-employment income of pensioners is currently exempt from national insurance contributions; the 22% rate is needed to prevent them paying more tax under my proposals.

The result would be equivalent to a net tax cut of £59.7bn, measured in a static way. I go on to provide a detailed explanation as to how the UK could afford this: I assume that 40% of the cuts in income tax, national insurance contributions and corporation tax will pay for themselves via stronger growth and less tax avoidance over three years; the rest would be partly compensated for by keeping nominal public sector spending growth to 2.5% a year for three years and reductions in wasteful spending, including the abolition of the Department of Trade and Industry. Transitionary financing would come from an acceleration in the government's privatisation programme, with the Post Office and some land holdings prime candidates for immediate disposal. Finally, I make the case that a little additional public borrowing during the transition period would not matter – it would be equivalent to an "investment" in a better tax system and better economy, just as Chancellor Gordon Brown is happy to "invest" in public sector capital spending.

This book is no more than a first, early and necessarily approximate analysis of a flat tax for the UK. Much more work needs to be undertaken, especially on modeling the impact and interaction of the flat tax combined with welfare reform; better data is also needed on the impact of the flat tax on Eastern Europe, which will only be available over time. But I believe this book, for all its inevitable limitations, to be by far the most comprehensive report yet published on the flat tax in Britain. It shows that – while undoubtedly a tricky endeavour – it would be possible and extremely desirable to go very quickly most of the way to a flat tax in the UK with the right political leadership.

Chapter II: The Hall and Rabushka pure flat tax model

Although the flat tax is not a new idea, it was developed and formalised for the first time by economists Robert E Hall and Alvin Rabushka – the second edition of their seminal work on the flat tax was published in 1995. It is important to understand from the outset that a flat tax is a much more complex system than merely a single-rate income tax. All other recent US proposals, including those of Dick Armey[26] and of Steve Forbes[27] are based at least in part on Hall-Rabushka; recent reforms are also inspired by that seminal work, even if not a single country has so far gone that far. The Hall-Rabushka flat tax is the purest form of the flat tax; it provides a benchmark against which reforms already in operation in countries around the world or proposals made by various think-tanks in the UK can be compared.

Hall-Rabushka go much, much further than the simple reforms that are often talked about in Britain. In addition to operating a single rate of tax on income above a personal allowance, it does away with the taxation of dividends, capital tax gains on equities and inheritance tax. Interest payments cease to be tax-deductible and capital spending becomes immediately deductible in year one, through a system of accelerated depreciation which sweeps away all of today's complex schedules.

Under Hall-Rabushka, all income generated in the economy is classified as either wages (salaries and pension income) or business income (everything else). The system is watertight and every form of income taxed only once and at exactly the same rate. Crucially, savings and investment are not taxed, which makes Hall-Rabushka an effective consumption tax for economic purposes, albeit one which is collected via an income tax system and which is able to help the poor by taking them out of taxes altogether thanks to generous personal allowances. This is the authors' explanation:

> *"We want to tax consumption. The public does one thing with its income – spends it or invests it. We can measure consumption as income minus investment. A really simple tax would just have each firm pay tax on the total amount of income generated by the firm less that firm's investment in plant and equipment. The value added tax works just that way. But a value added tax is unfair because it is not progressive. That's why we break the tax in two. The firm pays tax on all the income generated at the firm except the income paid to its workers. The workers pay tax on what they earn, and the tax they pay is progressive [thanks to the personal allowance]."* [28]

Under Hall-Rabushka, the current complex tax forms would be wiped away and replaced by two postcard-sized forms, which could obviously easily be filled in via the internet to

---

26 Armey, op. cit.
27 Forbes, op cit.
28 Hall and Rabushka (1995), op. cit, p55.

cut costs further. Everyone would have to fill in both forms. The first form – the personal income tax – would cover income from wages, salaries and pensions; the second – the business income tax – would cover all other forms of incomes. The business income tax would therefore be quite different from today's corporation tax, for good reason. As Hall and Rabushka put it in their book:

"The business tax is a giant withholding tax on all types of income other than wages, salaries and pensions. It is carefully designed to tax every bit of income outside wages but to tax it only once." [29]

Personal Income tax

The following represent the simple calculations that would go into working out the individual and company tax; they are largely self-explanatory.

FIGURE 1: PERSONAL INCOME TAX FORM UNDER A FLAT TAX

Line	Item	Figure	Calculation
1	Wages and salary	£	
2	Pension income and retirement benefit	£	
3	Total compensation	£	Line 1 + line 2
4	Personal allowance *	£	
5	Number of dependents excluding spouse		
6	Total personal allowances for dependents	£	Line 5 x personal allowance for dependents
7	Total personal allowances	£	Line 4 + line 6
8	Taxable compensation	£	Line 3 - line 4 if positive; otherwise zero
9	Tax	£	Flat tax % x line 8
10	Tax withheld by employer	£	
11	Tax due	£	Line 9 - line 10, if greater than zero
12	Refund due	£	Line 10 - line 9, if greater than zero

* In Hall-Rabushka, the personal allowance varies if married filing jointly, single, or single head of household

---

Lines 1 and 2 represent the income picked up by this tax; the other lines work out how much of the total income should be taxed at 0% and how much at the flat rate tax (in Hall-Rabushka, that's 19%). As Hall and Rabushka explain:

"The wage tax is not a complete income tax on individuals; it taxes only wages, salaries and pensions. The company business tax picks up all other components of income. Together they form an airtight tax system". [30]

One feature of this personal income tax form is that there is no line for allowable expenses. This is because under these proposals, jobs that generate expenses (such as freelance journalism or the operation of a mini-cab) would come under the business income tax form. Another feature is that there is no line for charitable deductions; most important of all, the flat tax allows no deductions for pensions.

In the UK, the personal income form would change little for the majority of the population, which today is on pay-as-you-earn and doesn't need to fill in a form. However, their employers would find their lives much improved and would be able to cut back on legal and payroll costs. People who have an additional income or who are not taxed on pay-as-you-earn would also benefit from an much simpler tax code.

Business income tax

The business tax is only a little more complex than the personal income tax. As the authors explain in their book, the forms of income it would tax include profits from the use of plant and equipment; profits from ideas embodied in copyrights, patents, trade secrets and other related items; profits from past organisation-building, marketing and advertising periods; the earnings of key people who are owners as well as employees of the company but who are paid less than they contribute to it; the earnings of professionals such as lawyers or accountants organised as proprietorships or partnerships; rent earned from commercial or residential property; and fringe benefits paid to workers.

---

30 Hall and Rabushka (1995), op. cit, p.60

FIGURE 2: BUSINESS INCOME TAX FORM UNDER A FLAT TAX

Line	Item	Figure	Calculation
1	Total proceeds	£	Proceeds from (a) sale of goods and services + (b) sale of capital equipment, structures and land + (c) self-employment income, partnership income
2	Total allowable expenses	£	(a) Purchases from other businesses of inputs required for production, including goods, services and materials + (b) salary, wages and pensions + (c) capital spending, including purchase of machines, property
3	Taxable income	£	Line 1 - line 2
4	Tax	£	Line 3 x flat tax %
5	Carry-forward from previous year	£	
6	Interest on carry-forward	£	Line 5 x interest rate
7	Carry-forward into current tax year	£	Line 5 + line 6
8	Tax due	£	Line 4 - line 7, if greater than zero
9	Carry-forward to next tax year	£	Line 7 - line 4, if greater than zero

The first line is straightforward as it represents the turnover of the company, as well as the proceeds from trading or asset disposals. They do not include capital gains on share trading, which are not taxed under the proposals. Lines 2-3 show what expenses can be subtracted from revenues. Crucially, line 4 does not represent corporate profits, as understood by the markets or accountants. A company that is having a great year in terms of accounting profits but that decides to spend a lot on capital expenditure would pay very little tax. Businesses would still produce their usual accounts under GAAP to allow shareholders and analysts to assess their performance and pre-tax profits.

Hall-Rabushka implies several major revolutions in the taxation of businesses. The first can be seen in line 2(c): it would allow the immediate expensing of all capital spending. It would accelerate depreciation dramatically, making it instantaneous; the very concept of depreciation would no longer be useful for the purpose of calculating taxes (it would still matter for profits).

Another revolution is that the form allows no expensing of interest payments – interest would no longer count as a cost to be subtracted from taxable profits. Companies and individual investors would no longer reap any tax advantage from borrowing.

At present, individuals pay tax on interest payments but corporate interest payments are deductible from tax: this means that interest is taxed only once. The difference under Hall-Rabushka is that the tax would be collected at the corporate level, rather than the individual level. In the UK, savings income is charged at 10% up to the starting rate limit, at 20% between the starting and basic rate limits and 40% above; under Hall-Rabushka, individuals would no longer pay any tax on interest but companies would no longer be able to deduct interest payments from tax. The economics would be the same (though the progressiveness would go); but the authors believe that their system is simpler and easier to manage – and it eliminates a key distortion in the economy in favour of greater corporate debt.

It is apparent from the two forms described above that certain types of income would no longer be taxable. These include dividends and capital gains on equities. At the moment, going against Hall-Rabushka, corporate profits are often taxed twice, dividends are discouraged and the tax system has a very strong in-built bias in favour of debt and against equity. Interest (i.e. payments on debt) is tax-deductible but dividends (payments on shares, or distributed profits) are taxed heavily. This is bad for corporate governance, reduces the returns on equity (the evidence is that high dividend shares perform better than low dividend shares over the long run) and encourages private equity firms (which leverage up and borrow huge amounts of money to take companies private) while discouraging stock market floats (which have a more prudent debt and equity mix).

Under the current UK tax code, profits are first taxed at the corporate level and then again when paid out as dividends to individuals. Dividend income is charged at 10% up to the basic rate limit of £32,400 and 32.5% above. This is partly offset by a dividend tax credit, which for those eligible can cut the effective rates to 0% and 22.5% respectively. For basic-rate taxpayers, company profits paid out as dividends are taxed once (via corporation tax on the company profits) rather than twice (via both corporation tax and income tax), which is what happens to dividends pocketed by top rate taxpayers.

A hypothetical large company which increases its profits by £100 and wants to pay the whole of this as a special dividend to its shareholders would first have to pay 30% corporation tax or £30 to the taxman, so it is left with £70, which it then hands out to its shareholders. Typically, these would be top rate taxpayers, paying at least 22.5% after the tax credit. In this simplified example, 22.5% of the £70 is £15.75 of the original profit after corporation tax. This means that of the £100 earned in profits, a total of £45.75 ends up in the coffers of Her Majesty's Revenues and Customs (HMRC), the successor organisation to HM Inland Revenue and HM Customs & Excise. The result is that distributed profits can face a marginal rate of tax of 45.75% or even more (for taxpayers ineligible for tax credits) under the current UK tax system, encouraging retention. Of course, companies make use of as many tax shields as they can, as do individuals, so they often pay less than this in tax.

Under a comprehensive flat tax, corporate profits would be taxed only once, at source. Individuals or institutions that own shares would pay no tax on their dividends; however, interest would cease to be treated as an expense and all other perks and tax breaks would be swept away. Tax would be payable on all profits, even for the smallest companies. The existence of tax on capital gains for equities is another instance of double-taxation which would be abolished under a comprehensive Hall-Rabushka flat tax. The price of a share is the net present value of its expected future cash flow, discounted at an appropriate risk-adjusted rate. A change in profits expectations is capitalised almost immediately by the markets; if expected profits increase by 10%, share prices tend to rise by the same amount. But because profits are already taxed when they occur at corporate level, and hence paid by the shareholders, taxing their reflection in the form of a capital gain would be a second tax on the same income and hence unfair.

Companies would continue to pay gain taxes on increases in the value of rental property, plant and machines, as would individuals, but all would be exempted on their shares. Individuals would continue to pay capital gains taxes on their second homes but first homes would be considered tax free – they are already taxed heavily under the guise of council tax and stamp duty, wealth taxes in all but name. The running of buy-to-let properties would be classified as a business activity.

There would obviously be losers as well as winners from a proper implementation of Hall-Rabushka, even if the population as a whole and the overall economy would benefit hugely. One set of losers from the proposed reforms are private equity firms and buy-out specialists that take companies private. They typically do so by borrowing large amounts of money and using the interest bill to slash taxable profits. Others who would be hit badly are buy-to-let investors, who are able to deduct mortgage interest payments for tax purposes from the rents they charge their tenants. There would be a good case for reform proposals to allow transition periods from the current system to the new one, especially for interest payments and past capital expenditure which hasn't yet been used against tax.

Even though Hall-Rabushka represents the purest model of a flat tax available anywhere, it is designed with an American audience in mind. It only applies to the US federal government – even though there is of course no real reason why state governments could not choose to raise all their revenues from an additional flat tax. At present, all US states, even those that currently have a single-rate state income tax, also levy others taxes, including sales taxes and property taxes in addition to income taxes. Americans don't have a value added tax, unlike every European Union country, including the UK. In practice, Hall-Rabushka is a tax on consumption and economically is therefore not that different from value added tax – with the crucial exceptions that VAT is invisible, doesn't damage incentives but is difficult to target while the flat tax remains progressive thanks to personal allowances.

Hall-Rabushka also deliberately ignores the social security payroll tax – which as it happens is flat, albeit not on all income – and allows it to continue existing unchanged. There is a very good reason for this: the US payroll tax is entirely earmarked to fund social security, the US state pensions system. None of the money it raises is used for other forms of government spending. Proposals for pension privatisation or reform, such as those of the Cato Institute or Heritage Foundation in Washington all involve individuals being allowed to divert part of their share of the social security tax into private accounts. This would eventually transform the US by creating a huge property-owning democracy, with funded pensions. Because of this, it makes sense for US tax reformers to leave social security well alone when drafting their own plans and to allow campaigners to push both plans separately.

But this is not necessarily true of the UK or of most European countries, including the Eastern European countries that have adopted their own versions of the flat tax. One of the greatest flaws in the way the British and most other governments currently tax personal income is that they rely on two parallel income taxes: the official income tax and national insurance contributions. The latter are supposedly a form of social insurance and a link remains between their payment and some state benefits. Opponents of the flat tax are right when they argue that the headline tax rates often cited in respect of Eastern European countries are misleading as they do not include often massive additional payroll taxes (though they are wrong that this invalidates the case for the flat tax).

In practice, in the UK, national insurance contributions are not truly earmarked and the money they raise is spent on whatever takes the government's fancy: they are therefore an income tax in all but name – the only difference being that they still formally entitle people who pay them to some benefits. But the only real reason the two systems continue to exist is that no government has either bothered or dared to merge them. This is partly because to do so would be to make the direct tax system more transparent; in the case of Gordon Brown, it has also allowed him to hike taxes on personal income, taking the top rate to a combined 41%, while sticking to the letter of Prime Minister Tony Blair's famous pledge prior to the 1997 general election not to put up income tax.

Some proposals for flat tax schemes devised by British commentators have ignored this major problem and focused instead only on official income tax. The same is true of the reforms actually implemented in Eastern Europe: they have all ignored national insurance contributions, which means that the real, effective marginal tax rates on employees are actually higher than the headline rates would suggest; it also means that employers' contributions, in effect a tax on employing people, also remain. As we shall see, a proper application of Hall-Rabushka in the UK context would include a merger of income tax and national insurance contributions; this is exactly what I propose be done in Chapter IX of this book.

Chapter III: The academic literature

Needless to say, Hall and Rabushka's proposals have prompted a large academic literature analysing and quantifying the gains to be had from adopting their proposals. Perhaps the most disappointing feature of the debate in the UK to date is the abject failure by critics (and even some supporters) to refer or take into account this burgeoning academic literature on the flat tax, mainly in US scholarly journals and central bank publications.

According to the Treasury's documents on the flat tax released under freedom of information legislation, "there is very little evidence that flat taxes work" and "heroic assumptions are made about economic gains which trickle down through the economy."[31] These are remarkable statements to make in light of the vast literature on the subject, the success of those countries that have already tried versions of the flat tax, let alone past instances of major tax cuts in the UK, US and other countries. It is also bizarre that (with the exception of a single study published by the International Monetary Fund[32]) one would be hard-pressed to find a single scholarly, peer-reviewed study on the flat tax by university academics that was cited or mentioned in the Treasury documents. Such a strange omission can only fuel fears that policy-making in Britain is being conducted in an appallingly amateurish fashion.

The biggest problem with the anti-flat tax claims from the Treasury and critics in think-tanks, investment banks, Universities and newspapers is their failure to acknowledge several essential sub-fields of economic research which ought to be compulsory reading to anyone interested in public policy. The first is the flat tax literature itself, starting with Hall and Rabushka's book. Others include the growing body of research examining the negative correlation between high taxes and economic growth[33]; studies quantifying how high tax rates reduce labour supply and entrepreneurial activity[34]; research arguing that government spending and especially high levels of government consumption (not merely high taxes) is bad for economic growth;[35] and the large scholarly literature arguing that economic freedom – measured by low public spending, low inflation, free trade, limited red tape and regulation, a strong commitment to property rights, a clear and predictable rule of law as well as low and simple taxes – is the essential driver of economic growth, productivity, wages and asset values.[36]

---

31 'Analysis and work carried out by HM Treasury or for HM Treasury on flat taxes', HM Treasury, 29 July 2005: http://www.hm-treasury.gov.uk/media/CFA/92/foi_flattax010805.pdf
32 Anna Ivanova, Michael Keen and Alexander Klemm, *The Russian Flat Tax Reform*, IMF Working Paper WP/05/16, International Monetary Fund: http://www.imf.org/external/pubs/ft/wp/2005/wp0516.pdf
33 For an excellent summary of some of the findings, see Graeme Leach (2003), *The negative impact of taxation on economic growth (Second Edition)*, Reform: http://www.reform.co.uk/filestore/pdf/negativeimpact.pdf ; see also '*Growth, Agenda for a reforming government*', Patrick Minford: http://www.cf.ac.uk/carbs/econ/minfordp/growthandtaxpaper10.pdf
34 Some of these papers are listed in Chris Edwards (2001), *Economic benefits of personal income tax reductions*, Joint Economic Committee, chaired by Jim Saxton , US Congress: http://www.house.gov/jec/tax/taxrates/taxrates.pdf
35 For a good review of the literature, see Daniel J. Mitchell (2005), *The Impact of Government Spending on Economic Growth*, Backgrounder No. 1831, Heritage Foundation: http://www.heritage.org/Research/Budget/bg1831.cfm
36 Further econometric confirmation and a survey can be found in Peter Gordon & Lanlan Wang (2004), *Does Economic Performance Correlate with Big Government?*, Econ Journal Watch, Volume 1, Number 2, pp. 192-221: http://www.econjournalwatch.org/pdf/GordonWangCommentAugust2004.pdf

We are still at a stage in the UK debate where commentators believe they can justifiably get away with not bothering to refute or attack any of the academic or model simulations with which they disagree – in fact, they still believe that it is acceptable simply to pretend that this body of work does not exist. The next step will be for these critics to track down one or two pieces of academic research which claims to have disproved the flat tax (using certain very specific assumptions) – and then to cite them over and over again as gospel and the definitive answer. This has already started to happen with the aforementioned IMF paper, which although a valuable contribution to the debate should no be seen as providing a definitive answer[37] as well as a paper from Lombard Street Research.[38] This simply will not do: if the UK Treasury wishes to be taken seriously, it will have to take seriously and attempt to rebut every single piece of contrary evidence, including the entirety of the literature cited in this book.

It is important to note at this stage that there are no longer any definitive answers to be found from modern economics, a profession which has tragically lost its way by trying to mimic physics. The extreme formalisation of the discipline, together with the inherent limitations of even the most advanced econometric tests, means that it is always possible to relax an assumption and to find a different result for almost any problem. Despite this important caveat, studying the professional literature remains important, if only to understand the state of the debate among academics.

Although opinions inevitably differ, a flat tax on the lines of that proposed by Hall and Rabushka – which as we have seen is a form of consumption tax that removes distortions from the graduations of the current income tax system and from the double taxation of capital income – is seen by many neutral university researchers as having strong positive effects on economic growth. Much of the academic literature finds as expected that there are important positive effects on capital accumulation, labour supply and welfare. At the same time, incomes become more unequal, which is also to be expected.

The best thorough review of the flat tax literature that I am aware of was compiled by Jason Clemens and Joel Emes with Rodger Scott in 2001 and published by the Fraser Institute in Canada.[39] The authors concluded that "These studies confirm that high and increasing marginal tax rates impede the formation of capital, retard economic growth, hinder per-capita income growth, and constrain aggregate labour supply. This seems a high price to pay for vertical equity and progressivity, which could be achieved with a flat tax." Not only does this conclusion still hold today, it has been reinforced further by the latest research.

Before reviewing a selection of the available research on the case for cutting marginal tax rates and introducing a flat tax, it is worth pointing out that there is also a large body of work making the case for a complete shift away from the taxation of

---

37 Ivanova, Keen & Klemm, op. cit.
38 See Chapter VII
39 Jason Clemens, Joel Emes with Rodger Scott, 'The flat tax—a model for reform of personal and business taxes', published as a chapter in Herbert Grubel [Editor] (2003), *Tax Reform in Canada: Our Path to Greater Prosperity*, The Fraser Institute: http://www.fraserinstitute.ca/admin/books/chapterfiles/Flat%20Tax-clemens_paper_1.pdf

income and capital towards the taxation of consumption; and an equally large amount of research making the case against the taxation of capital. There is simply not enough room to do any of this justice in the present publication.

The following scholarly research papers, which are unavoidably incompletely and superficially summarised, discuss the effects of cutting marginal tax rates on income and capital, introducing a flat tax and related issues. This is only to give readers a flavour of the debate; numerous additional academic papers are reviewed in subsequent chapters and are usually cited in footnotes.

- Auerbach and Kotlikoff (1987)[40]

This work calculates that the introduction of a Hall-Rabushka flat tax would raise the ratio of capital formation to GDP from 5.0% to 6.2% and boost the size of the economy by 2% to 4% within seven years.

- Reinhard and Kormendi (1989)[41]

The authors find that hikes in marginal tax rates hit economic activity, keeping average tax rates constant. This means that making a tax system less progressive while ensuring that the government makes the same amount in tax revenues as a share of the economy leads to faster economic growth and a bigger overall output. This confirms also that a government can increase its revenue by cutting marginal taxes – given the same tax to GDP ratio, if GDP goes up then taxes go up too.

- Lucas (1990)[42]

The abolition of capital income tax in this paper increases the capital stock by 30-34% and consumption by 6.7%.

- Plosser (1992)[43]

In this important paper, the author regresses the rate of growth of GDP per person against the income taxes to GDP ratio for OECD countries and finds a significant negative relationship.

40 Alan J. Auerbach and Laurence Kotlikoff (1987), *Dynamic Fiscal Policy*, Cambridge University Press, Cambridge
41 Reinhard B Koester & Roger C Kormendi (1989), *Taxation, Aggregate Activity and Economic Growth: Cross-Country Evidence on Some Supply-Side Hypotheses*, Economic Inquiry vol. 27(3), Oxford University Press, pp. 367-86: http://ideas.repec.org/a/oup/ecinqu/v27y1989i3p367-86.html
42 Robert E Lucas, Jr (1990), *Supply-Side Economics: An Analytical Review*, Oxford Economic Papers vol. 42(2), Oxford University Press, pp. 293-316: http://ideas.repec.org/a/oup/oxecpp/v42y1990i2p293-316.html
43 Charles I. Plosser (1992), *The search for growth*, Proceedings, Federal Reserve Bank of Kansas City, pp. 57-92: http://ideas.repec.org/a/fip/fedkpr/y1992p57-92.html

- Pecorino (1994)[44]

This paper lays out a model of growth through the accumulation of human capital and uses it to try and understand the effect of tax reform. It finds that "the growth rate effects of tax reform are found to be on the order of one percentage point of growth per capita. This gain in growth is associated with replacing the existing income tax structure with a consumption tax. Replacing the tax on physical capital with higher taxes on labour is found to be mildly growth reducing."

- Mullen and Williams (1994)[45]

The authors follow-up the work of Koester and Kormendi (1989) and calculate marginal tax rates for the American states. After holding all other factors constant they find that "lowering marginal tax rates can have a considerable positive impact on growth … creating a less confiscatory tax structure, while maintaining the same average level of taxation, enabling sub-national governments to spur economic growth."

- Feldstein (1995)[46]

Martin Feldstein, a prominent economist, argues that "a decrease in marginal tax rates causes not only an increase in labour supply (broadly defined), but also a shift in the form of compensation and a reduction in deductible expenses … Taxable income therefore rises substantially more than aggregate hours." Feldstein also discovers that the realisation of capital gains is extremely sensitive to changes in the rate of capital gains tax.

- Feldstein and Feenberg (1995)[47]

This superb paper calculates that Bill Clinton's misguided 1990s tax rise had a devastating effect on reported income. The 31% tax (at the time, the top rate, following earlier tax hikes under President George H.W. Bush) went up to 36% and a new top rate of 39.6% starting at $250,000 was also introduced. Feldstein and Feenberg discovered that top-rate taxpayers would have reported 7.8% more taxable income had the tax rates not been increased. This led the US government to lose more than half the extra revenue predicted by static analysis – in other words, assuming no behavioural changes. The authors argue that overall losses in efficiency associated from the hike (including the

44 Paul Pecorine (1994), *The Growth Rate Effects of Tax Reform*, Oxford Economic Papers vol. 46(3), Oxford University Press, pp. 492-501: http://ideas.repec.org/a/oup/oxecpp/v46y1994i3p492-501.html
45 John K. Mullen & Martin Williams (1994), *Marginal tax rates and state economic growth*, Regional Science and Urban Economics, Elsevier, vol. 24(6), pp. 687-705 http://ideas.repec.org/a/eee/regeco/v24y1994i6p687-705.html
46 Martin Feldstein (1995), *Behavioral Responses to Tax Rates: Evidence from the Tax Reform Act of 1986*, American Economic Review vol. 85(2), American Economic Association, pp. 170-74 http://ideas.repec.org/a/aea/aecrev/v85y1995i2p170-74.html
47 Martin S. Feldstein and Daniel R. Feenberg (1995), *The Effect of Increased Tax Rates on Taxable Income and Economic Efficiency: A Preliminary Analysis of the 1993 Tax Rate Increases*, National Bureau of Economic Research Working Paper No. W5370: http://ssrn.com/abstract=225433

impact on the supply of labour) was twice the paltry $8bn in extra money collected by the government following its fresh raid on US taxpayers.

- Eissa (1995)[48]

The author calculates that President Reagan's decision to slash the top tax rate from 50% down to 28% triggered an increase of female labour supply (+18% between 1984-1986 and 1990-1992). She says: "I find evidence that the labour supply of high-income, married women increased due to the Tax Reform Act of 1986. The increase in total labour supply of married women at the top of the income distribution (relative to married women at the 75th percentile of the income distribution) implies an elasticity with respect to the after-tax wage of approximately 0.8. At least half of this elasticity is due to labour force participation."

- Stokey and Rebelo (1995)[49]

The authors consider only tax systems in which the marginal tax rate is equal to the average tax rate. However, some of the assumptions they use are somewhat unrealistic. They find little impact from the introduction of a flat tax.

- Boskin (1996)[50]

Boskin estimates that a flat tax would boost "gross domestic product up to 10% higher per year by replacing the current corporate and personal income taxes with a broad-based, low-rate direct, or indirect tax on consumption or consumed income. Perhaps a conservative estimate would be 5% per year, which, however, is gained partly by forgoing some current consumption."

- Besci (1996)[51]

The author also follows-up on Koester and Kormendi (1989) to derive marginal tax rates for the American states. His research leads him to conclude that variations in the marginal tax rates charged by the different states of the US have a statistically significant effect on economic growth. He finds that "state and local taxes have temporary growth effects that are stronger over shorter intervals and a permanent growth effect that does not die out over time." He adds: "application of the new insights

48 Nada O. Eissa (1995), *Taxation and Labour Supply of Married Women: The Tax Reform Act of 1986 as a Natural Experiment*, National Bureau of Economic Research Working Paper No. W5023: http://ssrn.com/abstract=225802
49 Nancy L Stokey & Sergio Rebelo (1995), Growth Effects of Flat-Rate Taxes, *Journal of Political Economy* vol. 103(3), University of Chicago Press, pp. 519-50: http://ideas.repec.org/a/ucp/jpolec/v103y1995i3p519-50.html
50 Michael J. Boskin (1996), A Framework for the Tax Reform Debate, from Michael J. Boskin (Editor), *Frontiers Of Tax Reform*, The Hoover Institution: http://www-hoover.stanford.edu/publications/Selections/961/boskin.html (Abridged)
51 Zsolt Becsi (1996), Do state and local taxes affect relative state growth?, *Economic Review* issue Mar, Federal Reserve Bank of Atlanta, pp. 18-36: http://www.frbatlanta.org/frbatlanta/filelegacydocs/ACFD5.pdf

yields regressions in which relatively higher tax rates are found to have a significant negative effect on relative growth rates."

- Engen and Skinner (1996)[52]

This paper reviews numerous academic papers and finds that "a major tax reform reducing all marginal rates by 5 percentage points, and average tax rates by 2.5 percentage points, is predicted to increase long term growth rates by between 0.2 and 0.3 percentage points. Over a period of a little more than three decades, moving to a more efficient tax system would have meant a US economy $500bn larger than it actually was in 1996, which confirms that thanks to compounding even a small increase in growth leads to a massive bonus over a long period of time.

- Jorgenson and Wilcoxen (1997)[53]

Under a Hall-Rabushka type flat tax, "Labour supply increases sharply because the consumption tax raises real after-tax wages substantially at the margin. Household capital would decline by about 10% and business capital would increase by about 12%. GDP would increase by almost 3.3% in the first year relative to the base case due to the increase in labour supply." This would rise gradually to a peak of 3.7% and stabilise at 3.3% over the next quarter of a century.

- Leibfritz and Bibbee (1997)[54]

The authors regress the average growth rates between 1980 and 1995 for economies that are members of the OECD against average tax rates, marginal tax rates and average direct tax rates. They discover that a 10% in tax rates leads to a 0.5 point cut in the rate of growth, with the most damaging effects being inflicted by direct tax hikes.

- Auerbach, Kotlikoff, Smetters and Walliser (1997)[55]

The authors conclude: "moving to a flat tax that exempts capital income from taxation would substantially raise output and wages. Our model exhibits relatively large increases in the labour supply due to the reduction of progressivity in the tax schedules and, most importantly, due to the lump-sum tax on existing wealth when moving to full expensing.

52 Eric M. Engen and Jonathan S. Skinner (1996), *Taxation and Economic Growth*, National Bureau of Economic Research Working Paper No. W5826: http://ssrn.com/abstract=225613
53 Dale W. Jorgensen and Peter J. Wilcoxen (1997), *The Effects Fundamental Tax Reform and the Feasibility of Dynamic Revenue Estimation*, Paper prepared for the Joint Committee on Taxation's Symposium on Modeling the Macroeconomic Consequences of Tax Policy: http://wilcoxen.cp.maxwell.syr.edu/papers/jct.pdf
54 Alexandra Bibbee, Willi Leibfritz & John Thornton (1997), *Taxation and Economic Performance*, OECD Economics Department Working Papers 176: http://titania.sourceoecd.org/vl=3071603/cl=84/nw=1/rpsv/cgi-bin/wppdf?file=5lgsjhvj867l.pdf
55 Alan J. Auerbach, Laurence J. Kotlikoff, Kent A. Smetters & Jan Walliser (1997), 'Fundamental Tax Reform and Macroeconomic Performance', from *Two Papers on Fundamental Tax Reform*, Congressional Budget Office: http://www.cbo.gov/ftpdocs/2xx/doc266/twotax.pdf

Taxation of existing wealth reduces the consumption of all normal goods including leisure. Those increases in labour supply are likely to be greatly diminished if a consumption tax is combined with some kind of transition relief to ease the burden on people who hold existing assets."

- Carroll, Holtz-Eakin, Rider and Rosen (1998)[56]

The authors find that "a 5 percentage point rise in marginal tax rates would reduce the proportion of entrepreneurs who make new capital investment by 10.4%. Further, such a tax increase would lower mean capital outlays by 9.9%."

- Long (1999)[57]

The author finds a correlation between marginal tax rates and taxable income across American states, in a further confirmation of this powerful relationship. He finds that an increase in the marginal tax rate reduces taxable income and the rich as usual respond the most to changes in tax rates, declaring less income for higher rates and more for lower rates.

- Ventura (1999)[58]

This paper explores quantitatively the general equilibrium implications of a revenue neutral tax reform in which the current income and capital income tax structure in the US is replaced by a flat tax as in Hall and Rabushka (1995). The main results include (i) the elimination of taxation of capital income has an important and positive effect on capital accumulation; (ii) mean labour hours are relatively constant across tax systems, but aggregate labour in efficiency units increases. Households in the upper income quintile increase their labour hours by no less than 9%. Since these agents are highly productive, this latter effect explains the overall increase in the value of the aggregate labour input in efficiency units that is observed, which in turn reinforces the effect of higher capital levels on output.

- Caucutt, Imrohoroglu and Kumar (2000)[59]

"Experiments on a calibrated model indicate that the quantitative effects of moving to a

56 Robert Carroll, Douglas Holtz-Eakin, Mark Rider & Harvey S. Rosen (1998), *Entrepreneurs, Income Taxes, and Investment*, National Bureau of Economic Research Working Paper No. W6374: http://www.nber.org/papers/w6374.pdf
57 John E. Long (1999), *The Impact of Marginal Tax Rates on Taxable Income: Evidence from State Income Tax Differentials*, Southern Economic Journal Vol. 65, No. 4, pp. 855–869: http://apt.allenpress.com/aptonline/?request=get-abstract&issn=0038-4038&volume=065&issue=04&page=0855
58 Gustavo Ventura (1999), Flat tax reform: A quantitative exploration, *Journal of Economic Dynamics & Control* 23, pp.1425-1458: http://publish.uwo.ca/~gjventur/1202.pdf
59 Elizabeth M. Caucutt, Selahattin Imrohoroglu & Krishna B. Kumar (2000), *Does the progressivity of taxes matter for economic growth?*, Discussion Paper 138, Institute for Empirical Macroeconomics, Federal Reserve Bank of Minneapolis: http://www.mpls.frb.org/Research/dp/dp138.pdf

flat rate system are economically significant. The assumption made about the engine of growth has an important effect on the impact of a change in progressivity." Growth is boosted by up to 0.52 points in the simulations.

- Gruber and Saez (2000)[60]

This study has a remarkable and controversial conclusion: the optimal structure of marginal tax rates should be declining as you move up from lower to higher income brackets. The authors find that "the optimal tax system should feature declining (or at least not increasing) marginal rates."

- Clemens and Emes with Basham and Samida (2001)[61]

The authors use Statistics Canada's Social Policy Simulation Database and Model to quantify the changes in tax rates that would arise from the application in Canada of the principles of the personal income tax reform proposed by Hall-Rabushka. Assuming a simplified system with only personal and spousal exemptions, and child deductions, the federal flat tax rate required to raise the same amount of revenues as the current system is 18.3% with a provincial average rate of 10.3%. This implies an average personal income tax rate of 28.6%.

The authors argue that "When people decide to work an additional hour, to increase their human capital through education, or to invest their savings, they consider the marginal tax rate since it directly affects the proportion of increased income that accrues to them after they paid their taxes. The higher the marginal tax rate, the lower the return to productive activity and, thus, the lower the incentive for the individual, family, or business to engage in the additional productive activity. The folly of demanding higher marginal tax rates for those in the upper income brackets is that higher rates will create disincentives for the most productive members of society to increase their productivity. In so much as this reduces the economic growth that benefits all members of society, increases in marginal tax rates in the long run result cause all of us to be worse off than we might otherwise have been."

- Sillamaa and Veall (2001)[62]

The authors study the effect of Canadian tax cuts in the late 1980s. They find that lower

---

60   Jon Gruber and Emmanuel Saez (2000), *The Elasticity of Taxable Income: Evidence and Implications*, National Bureau of Economic Research Working Paper 7512: http://www.econ.berkeley.edu/users/saez/w7512.pdf
61   Jason Clemens, Joel Emes, Patrick Basham & Dexter Samida (2001), *Flat Tax: Principles and Issues*, Fraser Institute - http://oldfra er.lexi.net/publications/critical_issues/2001/flat_tax/index.html; and also Jason Clemens and Joel Emes with Rodger Scott (2001), *The flat tax—a model for reform of personal and business taxes*, published as a chapter in *Tax Reform in Canada: Our Path to Greater Prosperity*.http://www.fraserinstitute.ca/admin/books/chapterfiles/The%20Flat%20Tax%20%20A%20Model%20for%20 Reform%20of%20Personal%20and%20Business%20Taxes-04TaxReformClemensetalA.pdf
62   Mary-Anne Sillamaa & Michael R. Veall (2001), The Effect of Marginal Tax Rates on Taxable Income: A Panel Study of the 1988 Tax Flattening in Canada, *Journal of Public Economics*, Vol. 80, No. 3, pp. 341–56: http://socserv2.socsci.mcmaster.ca/~qsep/p/qsep354.pdf

marginal tax rates trigger greater income, but that this effect was less pronounced in Canada than it was in the US. The strongest surge in income following the tax cuts came from the self-employed, the elderly and the rich.

- Padovano and Galli (2001)[63]

The authors work on previous data to ensure that marginal tax rates are accounted for properly. They find that there is a negative correlation between high marginal tax rates and economic growth in the long-run.

- Altig, Auerbach, Kotlikoff, Smetters and Walliser (2001)[64]

This paper shows that adopting a Hall-Rabushka-style flat tax would boost long term output by 6%. The revenue-neutral flat-tax rate equals 22% initially and reaches 19.4% in the long run. The authors say: "The flat tax generates long-run utility gains across-the-board. Interestingly, the highest relative gains are for the richest and poorest lifetime-income groups."

- Jorgenson and Yun (2002)[65]

This paper calculates that if a Hall-Rabushka flat tax is introduced, the result will be welfare gains of at least $2.06 trillion, even after the flat tax is adjusted to make up for any revenue shortfall. If there are no revenue shortfalls or if they are met by a lump sum tax then the gains would be even greater.

- Aaronson and French (2002)[66]

The paper argues that "failure to account for wage-hours ties within a progressive tax system leads to an hours response to a change in marginal tax rates that may be biased downwards by as much as 10% for men and 17% for women". Individuals tend to supply more hours to the market when their wage is higher – and existing models wrongly underestimate this impact. The authors explain: "First, in a model where the wage is a function of hours worked, an increase in the post-tax wage resulting from a tax cut potentially leads to an increase in hours worked. This increase in hours worked leads to an increase in the pre-tax wage through the tied wage-hours effect, further escalating hours worked. Therefore, there is a larger labour supply response to a tax change than

63 Fabio Padovano and Emma Galli (2001), *Tax Rates and Economic Growth in the OECD Countries (1950–1990)*, Economic Inquiry, Vol. 39, No. 1 (January): http://ei.oxfordjournals.org/cgi/content/abstract/39/1/44
64 David Altig, Alan Auerbach, Laurence Kotlikoff, Kent Smetters, and Jan Walliser (2001), Simulating Fundamental Tax Reform in the United States, *American Economic Review*, Vol. 91, No. 3, pp.574-595: http://www.clevelandfed.org/Research/Workpaper/1997/wp9712.pdf
65 Dale W. Jorgenson and Kun-Young Yun (2002), *Lifting the burden: fundamental tax reform and US economic growth*, National Bank of Belgium working paper: http://www.nbb.be/doc/oc/repec/reswpp/WP21.pdf
66 Daniel Aaronson & Eric French (2002), *The Effects of Progressive Taxation on Labour Supply when Hours and Wages are Jointly Determined*, FRB of Chicago Working Paper No. 2002-22: http://ssrn.com/abstract=367175

to an equally sized wage change. Since most models do not account for tied wage-hours offers, the latter effect (i.e. the effect of increased hours worked on increasing wages, which should in turn further increase hours worked) is ignored. Therefore, this model misspecification problem causes tax analysts to understate the labour supply response to a tax change".

- Cassou and Lansing (2003)[67]

The authors decompose the growth effect of the reform into the parts attributable to the flattening of the marginal tax schedule, the full expensing of physical capital investment, and the elimination of double taxation of corporate dividends. Their model is inspired by Stokey and Rebelo (1995). They find that the most important growth-enhancing element is the flattening of the marginal tax schedule. While they find that a flat tax reform permanently increases per capita growth by up to 0.143 points per year, this relatively modest effect is due to their assumptions, including that the government would impose "higher average tax rate to pay for the more generous expensing and deduction features. This mitigates the resulting growth benefits." If this assumption were removed, then the growth advantages would be far greater.

- Chetty and Saez (2004)[68]

This paper analyses the effect of President Bush's dramatic cut to the tax on dividends in 2003 from a top rate of 35% to 15%. The authors discover a sharp and widespread surge in dividend distributions. The share of publicly traded firms paying dividends began to increase precisely in 2003 after having declined continuously for more than two decades. The report notes that "nearly 150 firms have initiated dividend payments after the tax cut, adding more than $1.5 bn to aggregate quarterly dividends. Most of these firms initiated regular, recurrent payments rather than one-time 'special' distributions". It also finds that many firms that were already paying dividends prior to the reform raised regular dividend payments significantly after the tax cut.

- Bohacek and Kejak (2004)[69]

The paper states: "Our simulation of the flat-tax reform increases the steady state levels by magnitudes found in the literature: capital stock increases by 30%, output by 10.8%, consumption by 4.6%, and welfare by 3.9%".

67 Steven P. Cassou and Kevin J. Lansing (2004), *Growth effects from shifting from a graduated rate tax system to a flat tax*, Economic Inquiry, Vol. 42, No. 2, pp. 194-213: http://www.frbsf.org/econrsrch/workingp/2000/wp00-15bk.pdf
68 Raj Chetty & Emmanuel Saez (2004), *Do Dividend Payments Respond to Taxes? Preliminary Evidence from the 2003 Dividend Tax Cut*, National Bureau of Economic Research Working Papers 10572: http://www.nber.org/papers/w10572.pdf
69 Radim Bohacek and Michal Kejak (2005), *Optimal Government Policies in Models with Heterogeneous Agents*, USC FBE Macroeconomics and International Finance Workshop: http://www.usc.edu/schools/business/FBE/seminars/papers/M_3-31-05_BOHACEK.pdf

- Scutella (2004)[70]

This paper examines the implications of moving to a system where benefits are universal and the marginal tax rates simplified to a constant rate, referred to as a basic income flat tax system. However, it finds that providing basic income levels that coincide with current benefit rates is costly, with a marginal tax rate of over 50% required for revenue neutrality.

- Diaz-Gimenez and Pijoan-Mas (2005)[71]

The authors use a general equilibrium model to quantify the effects of this type of reform for the US economy. They found that revenue neutral tax reforms may imply productivity and output gains but bring at the same time increases in the inequality statistics of the economy.

- Gonzalez and Pijoan-Mas (2005)[72]

This paper quantifies the macroeconomic and distributional implications of an array of flat tax reforms for Spain. It is noteworthy for being the first estimate of the quantitative implications of tax reform in Spain through the use of a fully specified dynamic general equilibrium model of individual behaviour. Using a model with heterogeneous agents, the authors find "that a revenue neutral reform with a marginal tax equal to 17.42% and a fixed deduction equal to 15% of per capita income will yield increases in aggregate consumption and labour productivity equal to 7.6% and 2.5% respectively." A revenue neutral flat tax reform with a marginal tax equal to 23.37% and a fixed deduction equal to 35% still displays aggregate gains and people in the lowest quintile of the wage distribution pay lower taxes and enjoy higher consumption than under the current income tax.

- Conesa and Krueger (2005)[73]

This paper computes the optimal progressivity of the income tax code in a dynamic general equilibrium model with household heterogeneity in which uninsurable labour productivity risk gives rise to a nontrivial income and wealth distribution. Using a utilitarian steady state social welfare criterion, the authors find "that the optimal US income tax is well approximated by a flat tax rate of 17.2% and a fixed deduction of about $9,400. The steady state welfare gains from a fundamental tax reform towards

---

70 Rosanna Scutella (2004), *Moves to a Basic Income-Flat Tax System in Australia: Implications for the Distribution of Income and Supply of Labour*, Melbourne Institute Working Paper No. 5/04: http://www.melbourneinstitute.com/wp/wp2004n05.pdf
71 J Diaz-Gimenez & J Pijoan-Mas (2005), *Evaluating Flat Tax Reforms in the U.S.*, Unpublished manuscript
72 Marta Gonzalez and Josep Pijoan-Mas (2005), *The Flat Tax Reform: a General Equilibrium Evaluation for Spain*, CEMFI Working Paper 0505: http://www.cemfi.es/~pijoan/articles/FlatTaxSp.pdf
73 Juan Carlos Conesa and Dirk Krueger (2005), *On the Optimal Progressivity of the Income Tax Code* http://www.wiwi.uni-frankfurt.de/professoren/krueger/opttaxescfs.pdf

this tax system are equivalent to 1.7% higher consumption in each state of the world." A majority of the population currently alive (roughly 62%) would experience welfare gains, suggesting that such fundamental income tax reform is not only desirable, but may also be politically feasible.

- Sialm (2005)[74]

This study demonstrates that there is a significant relationship between asset valuations and personal tax rates. Share prices tend to be higher when taxes are low and lower when taxes are high. "This result is consistent with the observation that stock and bond returns tend to be higher in periods when taxes decrease and lower when taxes increase", the paper argues, providing more evidence that tax reform would boost asset prices.

- St Etienne and LeCacheux (2005)[75]

According to an early version of the study seen by Laurence Boone, Barclays Capital's chief French Economist, St Etienne and LeCacheux report that overall the 1986 TRA increased taxation efficiency (by inducing people to declare properly their revenues thanks to lower marginal rates, as shown by the fall in tax reports that included the use of fiscal exemptions from 40% in 1986 down to 28% in 1989), and increased progressivity thanks to the reduction of fiscal exemptions that were mostly exploited by higher incomes.

---

74 Clemens Sialm (2005), *Tax Changes and Asset Pricing: Time-Series Evidence*, Working paper:
    http://papers.ssrn.com/sol3/papers.cfm?abstract_id=472226
75 C. St Etienne and J. LeCacheux (2005), *Rapport: Fiscalité de croissance*, Conseil d'Analyse Economique; 'Myths and Mysteries
    of flat tax systems', Laurence Boone, Barclays Capital, 8 September 2005

Chapter IV: Why tax rates are becoming flatter

The evidence

Tax systems are becoming flatter. Top rates of personal income tax, corporation tax, capital gains tax and taxes on dividends are falling. The case of Ireland is especially noteworthy. Western European nations have been reducing corporate tax rates in response to Ireland's 12.5 % rate, which was part of a package of supply-side tax cuts and reforms which propelled Ireland in the 1990s from being the "sick man of Europe" into a new "Celtic Tiger."

In 2000, 20 out of 30 major countries of the OECD had a higher corporation tax rate than Britain. Today, just five years later, only 10 do – and they are mostly in the slow-growth euro zone. According to KPMG's latest corporate tax rates survey, the overwhelming majority of countries that have changed their company tax rates have cut them since 2003. The trend is most pronounced in Europe, where Poland, Slovakia, Portugal and Ukraine cut their rates by 29.6%, 24%, 16.7% and 16.7% respectively. The average corporate tax rate fell to 29.96% for OECD countries, from 30.9% the year before; and to 31.32% for EU nations, from 31.84%.

In Latin America, the biggest cut was implemented in Costa Rica, where the tax rate was cut by 16.7% from 2003 to 2004, according to the KPMG research.[76] The average company tax rate in Latin America is 30.02% and in the Asia Pacific countries it is 30.37%. So these figures confirm that UK corporation tax rates are no longer internationally competitive.

The chart and tables below shows how the gap between the EU and UK has shrunk dramatically, despite cuts in the corporation tax rate in the UK to 30% from 33% under Chancellor Gordon Brown. Company tax rates have collapsed in the former Eastern European member states. Individual income tax rates have also fallen; Britain is one of the few to have seen an increase in tax rates following Chancellor Gordon Brown's 1-point increase in national insurance contributions on employees and employers, which took the top rate of personal income tax to an effective 41%.

---

76 'Global Tax: KPMG Corporate Tax Rate Survey' (2004)
http://www.us.kpmg.com/microsite/global_tax/ctr_survey/index.html

FIGURE 3: THE TOP COMPANY TAX RATE IS FALLING

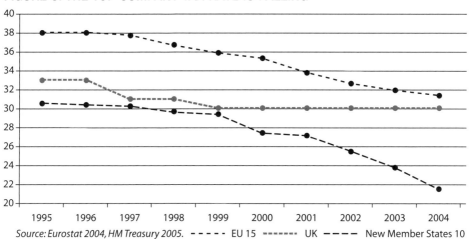

Source: Eurostat 2004, HM Treasury 2005.   - - - - - EU 15   - - - - - - - UK   - - - - New Member States 10

39

FIGURE 4: TOP MARGINAL INCOME TAX RATE FOR EMPLOYEES (SOURCE: OECD)

Country	Top marginal rates Combined 2000	Combined 2004	All-in 2000	All-in 2004	Statutory Income Tax Rate 2000	Statutory Income Tax Rate 2004	Threshold (multiple APW) (2) 2000	Threshold (multiple APW) (2) 2004	APW (3) 2000	APW (3) 2004	Threshold in $ (using PPP) (4) 2000	Threshold in $ (using PPP) (4) 2004
Australia	47.0%	48.5%	48.5%	48.5%	48.5%	48.5%	1.4	1.3	41,567	53,222	43,939	50,414
Austria	50.0%	42.9%	50.0%	42.9%	50.0%	50.0%	1.9	2.8	319,179	24,946	655,071	74,581
Belgium	52.6%	45.1%	65.7%	59.3%	60.5%	53.5%	2.6	1.2	1,169,841	32,281	3,259,382	41,422
Canada	44.7%	46.4%	44.7%	46.4%	44.7%	46.4%	2.0	2.8	36,982	40,912	63,504	94,682
Czech Republic	28.0%	28.0%	40.5%	40.5%	32.0%	32.0%	2.4	2.0	164,327	213,573	26,556	28,386
Denmark	54.3%	54.9%	63.3%	62.9%	59.7%	59.7%	1.1	1.0	282,600	327,192	36,515	38,166
Finland	52.6%	50.3%	59.8%	56.7%	55.2%	52.1%	2.2	2.0	153,600	29,449	340,804	60,363
France	47.3%	37.0%	48.1%	47.2%	61.3%	55.7%	6.2	3.4	136,500	23,087	913,236	87,691
Germany	53.8%	47.5%	53.8%	60.5%	53.8%	47.5%	2.0	1.6	62,377	34,088	125,521	56,911
Greece	45.0%	33.6%	45.0%	49.6%	45.0%	40.0%	4.9	2.2	3,557,014	12,525	25,139,950	38,450
Hungary	40.0%	56.0%	41.5%	69.5%	40.0%	38.0%	2.2	1.2	936,444	1,260,948	18,603	11,505
Iceland	43.1%	42.0%	43.1%	42.0%	45.4%	43.6%	1.5	1.5	2,247,855	2,859,073	34,710	44,642
Ireland	44.0%	42.0%	50.5%	48.0%	44.0%	42.0%	1.0	1.0	17,333	27,291	17,772	28,011
Italy	46.4%	41.4%	46.4%	51.6%	46.4%	46.1%	3.8	3.4	39,853,080	22,683	185,083,177	89,894
Japan	45.5%	47.1%	49.5%	47.8%	50.0%	50.0%	5.3	5.3	4,297,412	4,205,596	146,322	165,710
Korea	44.0%	36.6%	50.7%	39.2%	44.0%	39.6%	5.0	4.0	19,217,616	25,534,233	131,413	134,270
Luxembourg	47.2%	33.9%	47.2%	47.8%	47.2%	38.9%	3.0	1.3	1,179,930	32,586	3,535,442	40,560
Mexico	40.0%	26.6%	40.0%	28.9%	40.0%	33.0%	47.9	1.9	49,309	66,432	381,574	16,844
Netherlands	60.0%	52.0%	60.0%	52.0%	60.0%	52.0%	2.0	1.6	62,289	32,457	133,038	54,889
New Zealand	39.0%	39.0%	39.0%	39.0%	39.0%	39.0%	1.6	1.4	36,807	41,778	40,920	40,540
Norway	47.5%	47.5%	55.3%	55.3%	47.5%	47.5%	2.9	2.9	270,800	317,101	85,985	95,011
Poland	26.4%	26.2%	51.2%	51.6%	40.0%	40.0%	3.7	3.5	22,596	26,584	45,409	50,260
Portugal	35.6%	35.6%	46.6%	46.6%	40.0%	40.0%	4.9	6.7	1,532,224	8,905	11,395,009	87,686
Slovak Republic	36.6%	8.4%	49.4%	21.8%	42.0%	19.0%	12.8	0.5	104,263	180,000	83,731	5,352
Spain	48.0%	45.0%	48.0%	45.0%	48.0%	45.0%	5.0	3.0	2,495,112	17,913	16,597,544	66,415
Sweden	55.4%	56.5%	55.4%	56.5%	55.4%	56.5%	1.8	1.8	230,220	251,282	44,514	47,614
Switzerland	39.4%	37.8%	49.4%	47.9%	43.8%	42.1%	4.4	4.0	61,000	64,419	138,464	137,458
Turkey	35.6%	40.6%	35.6%	40.6%	40.6%	40.6%	5.9	10.6	5,545,029,433	13,670,289,738	119,221	702,270
United Kingdom	40.0%	40.0%	40.0%	41.0%	40.0%	40.0%	1.8	1.7	18,290	21,079	51,393	56,409
United States	46.7%	41.4%	48.1%	42.9%	46.5%	41.6%	9.6	9.4	30,918	34,934	296,813	327,049

FIGURE 4: Key to abbreviations: (Source: OECD)

Combined: The combined central government and sub-central government (top marginal) rate, calculated as the additional central and sub-central government personal income tax resulting from a unit increase in gross wage earnings. The combined rate takes account of the effects of tax credits, the deductibility of sub-central taxes in central government taxes etc.

Statutory: These are the statutory tax rates (combined central and sub-central) that apply at the threshold level reported in the fourth column.

All-in: The all-in (top marginal) tax rate, calculated as the additional central and sub-central government personal income tax, plus employee social security contribution, resulting from a unit increase in gross wage earnings. The all-in rate takes account of the same aspects as the combined rate, but does in addition include employee social security contributions and if they are deductible in central government taxes etc.

APW: Average production wage (in national currency), meaning the average annual gross wage earnings of adult, full-time manual workers in the manufacturing sector.

Threshold: The multiple of the APW earnings at which the reported combined top marginal rate is first observed.

Explanatory notes:

1. This table reports for each country the marginal combined personal income tax rate on gross wage income (derived according to the OECD Taxing Wages framework) for a single person without dependants based on the earnings level where the top statutory rate first applies. The third column shows the gross wage earnings threshold at which the top combined rate is met, measured as a multiple of the APW. The table also reports the 'All-in' rate at this threshold. The results, which use tax rates applicable to the tax year, take into account basic/standard income tax allowances and tax credits. The marginal tax rates are derived on the basis of a unit increase in gross wage earnings at the column 3 threshold. The reported marginal tax rate may not be the maximum possible marginal tax rate. A higher rate may be observed for higher income earners where tax allowance provisions may be diminished or eliminated as is the case in Belgium, France, Luxembourg, Mexico and Switzerland. A higher rate may also be possible at lower levels of income where there is a withdrawal of a tax relief as is the case in Italy, New Zealand, the United Kingdom and the United States. The figures reported may be different from those published in Taxing Wages where updated information is available, such as revised APW figures. Further explanatory notes may be found in the Explanatory Annex.

2. This column reports the level of gross wage earnings (expressed as a multiple of APW) at which the top marginal combined personal income tax rate is reached.

3. This column shows the average production wage, as described in OECD Taxing Wages.

4. This column shows the average production wage in USD, using OECDs purchasing power parity exchange rates.

FIGURE 5: CORPORATE INCOME TAX RATES

Country	Central government corporate income tax rate (2)		Adjusted central government corporate income tax rate (3)		Sub-central government corporate income tax rate (4)		Combined corporate income tax rate (5)		Targeted corporate tax rate (6)
	2000	2005	2000	2005	2000	2005	2000	2005	
Australia (a)	34.0	30.0	34.0	30.0			34.0	30.0	Y
Austria	34.0	25.0	34.0	25.0			34.0	25.0	N
Belgium	40.2 (39.0)	33.99 (33.0)	40.2	33.99			40.2	34.0	Y
Canada	29.1 (28.0)	22.1 (21.0)	29.1	22.1	15.5	14.0	44.6	36.1	Y
Czech Republic	31.0	26.0	31.0	26.0			31.0	26.0	Y
Denmark (b)	32.0	30.0	32.0	30.0			32.0	30.0	N
Finland	29.0	26.0	29.0	26.0			29.0	26.0	N
France (c)	37.76 (33.33)	34.95 (33.33)	37.8	34.95			37.8	35.0	Y
Germany (d)	42.2 (40.0)	26.375 (25.0)	35.0	21.9	17.0	17.01	52.0	38.9	N
Greece	40.0	n.a.	40.0	n.a.			40.0	n.a.	n.a
Hungary (e)	18.0	16.0	18.0	16.0			18.0	16.0	Y
Iceland	30.0	18.0	30.0	18.0			30.0	18.0	N
Ireland	24.0	12.5	24.0	12.5			24.0	12.5	Y
Italy (f)	37.0	33.0	37.0	33.0			37.0	33.0	N
Japan	30.0	30.0	27.4	n.a.	13.5	11.6	40.9	n.a.	Y
Korea	28.0	25.0	28.0	25.0	2.8	2.5	30.8	27.5	Y
Luxembourg	31.2 (30.0)	22.88 (22.0)	28.4	22.88	9.1	7.5	37.5	30.4	Y
Mexico	35.0	30.0	35.0	30.0			35.0	30.0	Y
Netherlands	35.0	31.5	35.0	31.5			35.0	31.5	Y
New Zealand (a)	33.0	33.0	33.0	33.0			33.0	33.0	N
Norway	28.0	23.75	28.0	23.75		4.25	28.0	28.0	Y
Poland f	30.0	n.a.	30.0	n.a.			30.0	n.a.	n.a.
Portugal	32.0	25.0	32.0	25.0	3.2	2.5	35.2	27.5	Y
Slovak Republic	29.0	19.0	29.0	19.0			29.0	19.0	Y
Spain	35.0	35.0	35.0	35.0			35.0	35.0	Y
Sweden	28.0	28.0	28.0	28.0			28.0	28.0	N
Switzerland (h)	8.5	8.5	6.38	6.45	18.54	17.65	24.9	24.1	N
Turkey	33.0 (30.0)	30.0	33.0	30.0			33.0	30.0	N
United Kingdom (a)	30.0	30.0	30.0	30.0			30.0	30.0	Y
United States (i)	35.0	35.0	32.7	32.7	6.7	6.6	39.4	39.3	Y

FIGURE 5: Explanatory notes: (Source: OECD)

1. This table shows 'basic' (non-targeted) central, sub-central and combined (statutory) corporate income tax rates. Where a progressive (as opposed to flat) rate structure applies, the top marginal rate is shown. Further explanatory notes may be found in the Explanatory Annex.

2. This column shows the basic central government statutory (flat or top marginal) corporate income tax rate, measured gross of a deduction (if any) for sub-central tax. Where surtax applies, the statutory corporate rate exclusive of surtax is shown in round brackets ( ).

3. This column shows the basic central government statutory corporate income tax rate (inclusive of surtax (if any)), adjusted (if applicable) to show the net rate where the central government provides a deduction in respect of sub-central income tax.

4. This column shows the basic sub-central (combined state/regional and local) statutory corporate income tax rate, inclusive of sub-central surtax (if any). The rate should be the representative rate reported in Table II.3. Where a sub-central surtax applies, the statutory sub-central corporate rate exclusive of surtax is shown in round brackets ( ).

5. This column shows the basic combined central and sub-central (statutory) corporate income tax rate given by the adjusted central government rate plus the sub-central rate.

6. This column indicates whether targeted (non-basic) corporate tax rates exist (e.g., with targeting through a special statutory corporate tax rate applied to qualifying income, or through a special deduction determined as a percentage of qualifying income). Where a 'Y' is shown, more information can be found in Table II.2.

Country-specific footnotes:

(a) For Australia, New Zealand and the UK, all with a non-calendar tax year, the rates shown are those in effect as of 1 July, 1 April and 5 April, respectively.

(b) In December 2004, the government put forward a proposal to reduce the central government corporate income tax rate from 30 per cent to 28 per cent with effect from 1 January 2005. The bill has not yet been adopted by the parliament and the proposal must be reintroduced after the recent election.

(c) These are the rates applying to income earned in 2000, to be paid in 2001. The rates include surcharges, but does not include the local business tax (Taxe professionnelle) or the turnover based solidarity tax (Contribution de Solidarité). More information on the surcharges is included as a comment.

- These are the rates applying to income earned in 2005, to be paid in 2006. The rates for 2005 are subject to final approval in Loi des Finances Initiale pour 2006 and Loi des Finances Rectificative pour 2005. The rates include surcharges, but does not include the local business tax (Taxe professionnelle) or the turnover based solidarity tax (Contribution de Solidarité). More information on the surcharges is included as a comment.

(d) The rates include the regional trade tax (Gewerbesteuer) and the surcharge.

(e) The rates does not include the turnover based local business tax.

(f) These rates do not include the regional business tax (Imposta Regionale sulle Attività Produttive; IRAP). See explanatory notes for more details.

(g) Source for the information: KPMG's Corporate Tax Rate Survey.

(h) Adjusted central and sub-central tax rates are calculated by the Swiss Federal Tax Administration (see 'Quels taux effectifs et nominaux d'imposition des sociétés en Suisse pour le calcul des coins fiscaux. Le procédé de la déduction fiscale en Suisse'). Church taxes are included, but the results excluding church taxes are indicated as comments.

(i) The sub-central rate is a weighted average state corporate marginal income tax rate. See explanatory notes for more details.

Tax competition

The spread of the flat tax from Eastern Europe to Western Europe is probably the most stunning illustration of how economies in a globalised economy with limited barriers to trade and investment, no capital controls and increasing mobility of skilled and high-net worth workers, are increasingly competing with each other to attract capital and labour. Economists have confirmed that this process – dubbed tax competition – is a key cause of lower tax rates and that countries compete especially on their statutory tax rate and effective average tax rate.[77] It explains the evidence described above.

Erik Nielsen, an economist at Goldman Sachs, says: "Policy competition from the new EU members in Central Europe has already set the train in motion, and will lead to reforms of fiscal policies as well as further labour and product market deregulation in Old Europe. As such, the ten new EU members, with only about 5% share of EU's GDP, are punching way above their weight when it comes to their influence on European policymaking. In a globalised world of free capital (and increasingly free labour) mobility, that is good news for Europe".[78]

He argues that the process of simplification of the tax regimes towards lower rates has begun, regardless of who wins particular elections, and this is good news for European productivity and growth. However, the process of tax competition began in earnest in the 1980s when the US and UK slashed their top tax rates under President Ronald Reagan and Prime Minister Margaret Thatcher. In the 1990s, Ireland's low tax policy and 12.5% corporate income tax also had an important influence.

Several Nobel Prize winners in economics have recently given tax competition their full support.[79] James Buchanan, who won the prize in 1986, said: "...tax competition among separate units...is an objective to be sought in its own right." Milton Friedman, the 1976 winner, said: "Competition among national governments in the public services they provide and in the taxes they impose is every bit as productive as competition among individuals or enterprises in the goods and services they offer for sale and the prices at which they offer them." Gary Becker, who won in 1992, said: "...competition among nations tends to produce a race to the top rather than to the bottom by limiting the ability of powerful and voracious groups and politicians in each nation to impose their will at the expense of the interests of the vast majority of their populations."

According to Nielsen, tax competition has three positive effects which directly improve productivity and growth[80]:

---

77 Michael P. Devereux, Ben Lockwood, and Michela Redoano (2002), *Do Countries Compete Over Corporate Tax Rates?* mimeo, University of Warwick: http://www2.warwick.ac.uk/fac/soc/csgr/research/workingpapers/2002/wp9702.pdf
78 'Europe: Getting Ready for Lower, Flatter and Simpler Taxes', Erik F. Nielsen, *European Weekly Analyst*, Issue No: 05/34, 8 September 2005, Goldman Sachs
79 See '*Tax Competition as a Means to Control Leviathan*', Daniel J Mitchell, Presentation to Mont Pelerin Society, Reykjavik, Iceland, 24 August 2005
80 Nielsen, op. cit.

- By eliminating complex features of the tax code, such as excessive numbers of tax brackets and exemptions, "the administrative burden of managing taxes declines, both for the public and private sectors, thus releasing resources for more productive activities in the countries that spearhead the move."

- The "announcement effect" of tax simplifications sends important messages about the government's overall reform agenda to businesses, and may thus encourage additional investment by global and local firms.

- It impacts potential moves in the tax base. While labour remains considerably less mobile than capital, it is not zero, partly because personal income tax rates has an effect on the location of foreign investment as well as on skilled workers.

Fresh evidence that the flattening of tax rates is good for growth keeps accumulating. In a paper published in June 2005 in the prestigious Journal of Public Economics, two academic economists explore how tax policies affect a country's growth rate, using cross-country data for 1970–1997.[81] They find that corporate tax rates are significantly negatively correlated with economic growth, controlling for other determinants of economic growth, and other standard tax variables. Increases in corporate tax rates lead to lower future growth rates within countries. A cut in the corporate tax rate by 10 percentage points will raise the annual growth rate by one to two percentage points, the authors find. And as we have already seen, there is plenty of other evidence to show that the same is true of income tax and taxes on capital as well. Governments may not like to have to cut tax rates but it is great news for growth, jobs and wages that tax competition is forcing them to do so.

Tax competition has become the essential counter-balance to the highly organised pressure groups that have become so influential in Western democracies. These groups make use of the fact that the cost in terms of higher taxation for the average voter of an extra spending plan is tiny and almost imperceptible – but the advantages of each new spending plan tend to be highly concentrated and benefit a small number of people in an important and very noticeable way. It is a case of dispersed costs and concentrated benefits, which gives taxpayers little incentive to organise to lobby for lower taxes but gives interest groups a very strong incentive to band together to campaign for more spending. Combined with what political scientists call the 'rational ignorance' of much of the electorate – it doesn't pay for most people to find out what is going on, they are better off free-riding on others – there is a built-in ratchet on public spending, which means that it is never cut and always increased.

81 'Tax structure and economic growth', Young Lee and Roger H. Gordon, *Journal of Public Economics*, Volume 89, Issues 5-6 , June 2005, Pages 1027-1043

The only real counterweight to this is tax competition. If countries put up their tax rates too high, capital and skilled labour flows out. This forces governments to keep their domestic spending lobbies in check or at least to reorganise their tax collection in ways that minimise the damage to their economies (such as by moving away from taxes on capital and increasing taxes on consumption instead). This pressure is an important explanation for why the flat tax has been gaining so much ground in Eastern Europe. As Daniel J. Mitchell, a senior fellow at the Heritage Foundation, puts it: "Organised interest groups often pressure governments to impose high tax rates and create tax biases against capital. Tax competition creates an offsetting pressure, thus encouraging governments to implement pro-growth tax policy."

Tax protectionism

Nevertheless – and all too predictably – the world's three largest international bureaucracies have tried to fight back and crush tax competition, which they realise will constrain the ability of countries to tax as they want. These organisations are acting like producer cartels: no wonder they have been dubbed by some critics an "Opec for tax-hungry politicians".[82]

The most prominent campaign to reduce tax competition is that waged by the Organisation for Economic Co-operation and Development, which launched its "harmful tax competition" initiative in the 1990s, identifying more than 40 so-called tax havens and threatening them with sanctions and financial protectionism unless they weaken their tax and privacy laws.[83] There are also various 'corporate governance' and 'flags-of-convenience' campaigns.

The OECD acknowledges that competitive forces have encouraged countries to make their tax systems more attractive to investors. However, it argues, some tax practices are "anti-competitive and undermine fair competition and public confidence in tax systems", which is why it wants to crack down on the practice. It adds: "OECD and non-OECD economies are working together through the Global Forum to address harmful tax practices by improving transparency and establishing effective exchange of information."[84] The truth, of course, is that this crackdown on jurisdictions with low taxes has less to do with fighting crime and terrorism than it has to do with economic protectionism and a desire by rich countries to rig the market in their favour.

There has, however, been dissension in the ranks of the OECD, with some economists writing that "the ability to choose the location of economic activity offsets shortcomings in government budgeting processes, limiting a tendency to spend and tax

82 For papers making the case for tax competition, see 'Harmful Tax Competition', Richard Teather, *Economic Affairs*, December 2002: http://www.teather.me.uk/pubs/pubs0008.pdf; '*Multinational tax competition: A legal and economic perspective*', Richard Teather, Tax Research Network, Cambridge University, September 2002: http://www.teather.me.uk/pubs/pubs0004.htm
83 Daniel J. Mitchell, *The Economics of Tax Competition: Harmonisation vs. Liberalisation*, chapter 2 of *The 2004 Index of Economic Freedom*, Heritage Foundation
84 Harmful Tax Practices, OECD: http://www.oecd.org/topic/0,2686,en_2649_33745_1_1_1_1_37427,00.html

excessively"[85] and that "legal tax avoidance can be reduced by closing loopholes and illegal tax evasion can be contained by better enforcement of tax codes. But the root of the problem appears in many cases to be high tax rates."

In the European Union – including of course the UK and Ireland, as well as the new Eastern European member states – numerous tax harmonisation proposals such as the savings tax directive and plans to harmonise corporate tax base and eventually tax rates are clearly intended to erode and destroy tax competition. The EU has scored some notable successes – in particular, member states have lost control of VAT rates, which must usually remain between 15% and 25%, with some exceptions.

One of the EU's main projects has been the savings tax directive, to require countries to impose a tax on foreign investors (who own bank accounts or government bonds in another country) and turn the money over to the investor's government; or to gather information about these investment earnings and exchange them with other governments.

Despite the welcome defeat of the EU constitution in 2005 following No votes in referenda in France and the Netherlands, the threat of EU tax harmonisation remains. It is likely to continue to be driven by the European Court of Justice; supporters of a flat tax and lower taxes in the UK will sooner or later have to realise that membership of the EU is a long-term threat to their policies.

Meanwhile, euro zone politicians including Germany's former Chancellor Gerhard Schröder have accused Eastern European flat tax countries of stealing business with their low tax rates while at the same time pocketing handouts from Brussels. Last year, would-be French President and current government minister Nicolas Sarkozy said that if the new states were "rich enough" to introduce a flat tax they wouldn't need EU funds. The handouts are of course destructive; but their abolition should not be linked to the adoption of a flat tax by some of its recipients. France and Germany are the two main EU countries which have been the most open about calling for wholesale tax harmonisation in a bid to crush tax competition and destroy the competitive advantage of Eastern Europe.

Supporters of tax harmonisation in the EU tend to be on the political left and usually claim that high tax rates do not damage growth. However, these same people also often claim that differences in tax rates across nations will damage the international allocation of resources by distorting choices. But to hold these two positions simultaneously is contradictory: either people do not respond to high taxes or they do.

The United Nations is also trying to grab a slice of the harmonisation action. It would like to create an International Tax Organisation with the power to override national governments and prevent tax competition.[86]

85 OECD, *Economic Outlook*, No. 63 (June 1998).
86 Daniel J. Mitchell (2001), *United Nations Seeks Global Tax Authority*, Prosperitas, Vol. I, No. II
    http://www.freedomandprosperity.org/Papers/un-report/un-report.shtml

Chapter V: The advantages of flatter taxes

Goodbye, pen pushers

One of the most important advantages of a flat tax – and the one that usually appeals most to the general public when they are introduced to the idea– is that it would sweep away bureaucracy and dramatically cut the compliance costs of raising revenues for the state. In a now famous interview for the New York Daily News in 1997, the actor and entertainer Clint Eastwood, explained how the world would suddenly change if politicians adopted a flat tax: "All of a sudden, what do you have? You have the whole tax system run by a little old lady on a home computer, doing the work of all these thousands of bureaucrats and accountants. Passing that would be amazing, wouldn't it?"[87]

Crucially, the wealthy would no longer have an incentive to hire accountants to exploit tax loopholes as these would no longer exist; many tax lawyers, financial consultants and other members of the tax industry would have to find a more productive way of making a living. Cutbacks could also be made to HMRC, which has a budget of £4.6bn in 2005-06: a large chunk of this could be eliminated under a flat tax.

In Britain, the tax code is now of Byzantine complexity and has exploded since the arrival to 11 Downing Street in 1997 of Gordon Brown, a man who seems to love making simple things as complicated as possible. If a flat tax were adopted, the bulk of the tax code would be torn up and tax forms would fit onto a postcard. US flat tax advocates have produced drafts and flat tax calculators available on the Internet.[88]

By 1997 the British tax code took 4,555 pages to explain, the result of about 200 years of tax law. It has taken Chancellor Gordon Brown just 8 years to practically double that to 9,050 pages, according to the latest edition of Tolley's Yellow Tax Handbook, which contains the entirety of UK direct taxation legislation for 2005-06 and is the tax accountant's Bible. This includes all Statutes, Statutory Instruments and Inland Revenue Statements of Practice and Extra-Statutory Concessions, although the latter two categories have been used sparsely in recent years. The combined May and August 2005 editions cost £120 from LexisNexis Butterworths[89] and are utterly incomprehensible to anybody other than a specialist accountant or tax lawyer.

As Erik Nielsen of Goldman Sachs puts it: "Along with gradually higher tax rates, exemptions have mushroomed throughout Europe. As a result, what were originally intended as progressive tax systems have become highly opaque systems, and may in some cases even have become regressive. Moreover, the complexity of multiple tax brackets and hundreds of exemptions has created a significant administrative burden in managing the system, both for the public sector and for individuals, and in turn has given

---

87 *New York Daily News*, op. cit.
88 See for instance the flat tax calculator at http://www.cse.org/flattax/index.php
89 'Yellow and Orange Tax Annuals', *LexisNexis*, August 2005
    http://www.lexisnexis.co.uk/attmembersoffer/yellow_tax_handbook.html

rise to a fundamentally unproductive sector of tax advisers"[90].

The Institute of Chartered Accountants in England & Wales (ICAEW), the main trade body for UK accountants, has highlighted the phenomenal increase in tax legislation over the past twenty-five years – recording a 54% increase in the number of pages in the Finance Acts in the last five years alone and a threefold increase since the early 1980s. The research follows the recent publication of the second Finance Act of 2005.

In the 2000-2005 period, the average number of pages in each year's Finance Acts was 481 compared with an average of only about 157 in the early part of the 1980s. The Finance Acts today are more than three times as big as they were twenty-five years ago and over each five-year period the increase in the number of pages has never been less than 17%. The most recent five-year period has seen an increase of over 50% over the previous five-year period.[91]

Lord Roberts of Conwy, speaking in a recent House of Lords debate, said: "The Inland Revenue's budget has doubled in real terms in the five years to 2004. The number of pages in the Finance Act averaged 346 from 1987 to 2003. The 2004 Finance Act was 634 pages long. Membership of the Chartered Institute of Taxation has grown by 42% in the past decade. All of this gives us some idea of the growth in the complexity of the UK tax system".[92]

The ICAEW is one of several leading groups to be campaigning for tax simplification. Its arguments, available on its website, are cogent and show that even tax professionals – who are often thought to have a vested interest in complex taxes – understand the need for greater simplicity. "The UK tax system is spiraling out of democratic control. The speed with which much new legislation is introduced leaves little or no time for consideration of the issues nor allows for second thoughts and useful amendments. This compounds the complexity of a system which has developed in such a way that even highly numerate taxpayers are struggling to understand the tax implications of their actions. Frequent changes to the tax legislation only compound the problem." The ICAEW goes on to argue that because of the complexity of the current system, business decisions are inhibited and become more expensive not only in terms of compliance costs but also in terms of time spent dealing with tax issues, increasing the costs of economic activity. The ICAEW adds: "Equally, individual taxpayers have to bear a heavy compliance burden. In turn, inhibited economic activity reduces national income and decreases Government revenues. With real political will the way we introduce new tax law can be reformed. The prize of reform will be threefold: freer economic activity, increased national wealth and greater revenue for Government."[93]

The ICAEW believes that all taxpayers should be entitled to understand why they

---

90 Nielsen, op. cit.
91 'Tax legislation is toppling Big Ben says Institute of Chartered Accountants':
    http://www.icaew.co.uk/cbp/index.cfm?AUB=TB2I_86111%7CMNXI_86111&CFID=107739&CFTOKEN=93781084
92 'Tax Flat rate - Tax: going flat out', 26 September 2005, *Accountancy*
93 '*Tax Simplification*', Institute of Chartered Accountants for England and Wales,
    http://www.icaew.co.uk/index.cfm?AUB=TB2I_55564IMNXI_55564

are being taxed, on what they are being taxed and how that tax is calculated; certainty and consistency in taxation; and to know that the costs of complying with their tax responsibilities are being kept to an absolute minimum. All three of these points are well-made and should be part of any British flat tax plan.

The ICAEW also adds several proposals, some of which should also be adopted. The government should challenge the assumption that changes to tax policy should be made every year. Instead, it should undertake only to alter tax legislation when such change is clearly necessary. The government should also publish its estimates of the full costs and benefits of any new tax legislation, justifying its introduction with evidence. It should also consult on all major tax issues, giving adequate time for views to be considered and providing detailed feedback on the results of the consultation.

Even HMRC (sometimes) recognises the problems caused by complexity. "Whilst addressing perceived complexities in the tax regimes is not for this review, the links between complexity and compliance need to be recognised. Complexity can lead to incorrect returns where it leaves too much scope for different interpretations and can also hinder timely filing".[94]

The United States spends between 10% and 20% of the annual revenue collected on the administration and enforcement of its progressive tax structure which equates to between one-quarter and one-half of the government's budget deficit.[95]

The UK Treasury has also admitted that "with only one rate and minimal, if any, credits or exemptions to calculate, the administrative burden on governments is considerably reduced. In progressive tax structures, the administrative cost and compliance burden are considerable. This cost should be significantly lower in flat tax structures, increasing the spending power of the tax raised."[96] True to form, however, the mandarins immediately added the following caveat: "Unfortunately, no raw data exists to date to support this claim given the lack of studies on existing flat tax structures to date."

Predictability, transparency and privacy

In their consultation document on tax reform, the Liberal Democrats rightly point out that predictability is an important virtue of a tax system. "If the government has long term objectives for tax reform, it is better that these are openly stated and pre-announced even if they are to be implemented over a number of years, rather than introduced piecemeal with no strategic plan. Especially where tax changes are meant to influence behaviour and investment decisions, evidence of a long tem commitment to the direction of reform will be important", they argue.

But predictability should also be about more than merely a transparent reform process: with a flat tax, the overall tax system would be far more predictable because a

---

94 HM Revenue and Customs and the Taxpayer – Consultative Committee Meeting, 6th July 2005
95 *The Economist,* 16 April 2005.
96 HM Treasury, op. cit.

committed government would in effect bind itself to maintaining a flat system, and so taxpayers and investors would be relatively confident that changes would remain within strict bounds.

In a country where a flat tax is well established and accepted as the norm by the population, a government that decides to increase taxes would have to be very open about it. It would have to either reduce the personal allowance or increase the single tax rate – making the cost of its policies obvious to all. A flat tax would make it much harder to introduce the kind of stealth tax favoured by Gordon Brown.

In recent years, there have been increasing tensions between the government and big companies as a result of Brown's drive to crack down on tax evasion. Many business leaders are angry at what they believe are in fact tax increases by another name and by the fact that this has created a lot of uncertainty as to what the tax laws really are. The latest crackdown on avoidance, which is supposed to bring in an extra £3bn over the next three years, is based on significant changes on HMRC's interpretation of the tax law – and could therefore be seen to be a change in the law itself, perhaps even a retroactive one. Such behaviour is neither compatible with traditional notions of natural justice nor conducive to an efficient and simple tax system; it would be ruled out under a well-established flat tax with a broad and clear base.

A central problem with the current tax system is the degree of government snooping that is required to make it work. A simpler system where many taxes such as those on inheritance no longer exist would significantly reduce the amount of private information individuals would have to hand over to government officials. A tax system that fits on a simple form would be far more respectful of privacy. By significantly reducing tax avoidance and the use of foreign tax havens, policies such as the European Unions' information exchange deals between national governments would become redundant.

Reducing deadweight losses

Each extra pound raised in taxes ends up costing the economy much more than a pound. This extra burden is attributable not only to compliance and administrative costs but also to what economists call deadweight losses, a somewhat nebulous concept but one that is crucial to understanding basic microeconomics.[97] Also sometimes called an excess burden, a deadweight loss occurs when individuals change their behaviour in response to higher taxes, reducing economic welfare measured by the consumer and producer surplus.

In its February 2001 Budget Options report, the US Congressional Budget Office notes that "typical estimates of the economic cost of a dollar of tax revenue range from

---

97 For an explanation, see any introductory microeconomics textbook. Edwards (op. cit) is very useful on the subject. An excellent review of the literature and estimates on the size of deadweight losses is contained in Graeme Leach (2003), *The negative impact of taxation on economic growth* (Second Edition), Reform: http://www.reform.co.uk/filestore/pdf/negativeimpact.pdf

20 cents to 60 cents over and above the revenue raised."[98] In other words, the real cost to the economy of a £10 tax hike is between £12 and £16 when the additional visible and invisible costs of economic distortions is factored in; in the same way, the real benefit of a £10 tax cut is greater than £10. This further weakens the case for tax hikes and increases that for tax cuts. Needless to say, one will not find acknowledgments of the deadweight cost of tax – such as the estimates from the US Congressional Budget Office – in any publication from the UK Treasury.

Income tax systems with increasing marginal tax rates compound the deadweight loss created by all taxation (with the exception of the largely theoretical concept of lump-sum taxes, defined as taxes that do not affect behaviour in any way). Economists agree that the deadweight losses to the economy go up more than proportionally with tax rates, which further strengthens the case for a flat tax.

The deadweight loss caused by a tax is not necessarily synonymous with any reduced economic growth it may cause. In economics, deadweight costs attempt to measure any reductions in welfare or utility suffered by individuals; economic growth excludes many ways by which individuals derive utility, especially leisure. If people were to work harder in response to a tax increase, as some left-wing economists have implausibly claimed they may do (in technical terms, this would mean that the income effect of the tax hike is greater than its substitution effect), their welfare would be reduced even if output stays the same because they will have to sacrifice some of their leisure. In practice, however, higher taxes on income and capital reduce economic output and also reduce welfare and increase deadweight losses.

The existence of deadweight losses is a key argument for a flat tax. This is because the losses rise more than proportionally to rises in tax rates: the formula used by economists is that deadweight losses increase roughly by the square of the increased tax wedge between pre-and post tax income. So a flat tax would massively reduce the deadweight loss of raising tax revenues.

As leading US economist Chris Edwards writes in a recent Joint Economic Committee paper, a doubling of the tax wedge causes deadweight losses to quadruple; "as a consequence, a flatter tax rate structure is substantially more efficient than a progressive tax structure that has rising marginal rates".[99] Even small cuts in marginal tax rates can do wonders for economic efficiency. One study found that deadweight losses are worth about 18% of total US tax revenues and 39% of all additional revenues raised.[100] A paper by prominent US economist Martin Feldstein found that the deadweight loss was worth 32% of income tax revenues in the US but 78% of additional revenues.[101] Given that Britain's income tax system is even more steeply graduated than that of the US, deadweight losses in the UK are likely to be even greater.

98 Cited in Edwards, op cit.
99 Edwards, op. cit.
100 'The Excess Burden of Taxation in the United States', Dale Jorgenson & Kun-Young Yun, *Journal of Accounting, Auditing, and Finance*, Fall 1991.
101 Martin Feldstein (1995), *Tax Avoidance and the Deadweight Loss of the Income Tax*, NBER Working Paper 5055, March.

Boosting incentives

Discussions of tax policy constantly revolve around a small number of important concepts. A critical distinction is made between the average or effective tax rate on the one hand and the marginal or incremental tax rate on the other. The former term denotes the average proportion of income that must be handed over to the government in taxes; the latter the proportion of any additional income that must be given up. A second vital distinction is made between tax rates and tax revenues: tax rates may go up and tax revenues simultaneously go down; and vice-versa.

Marginal tax rates are more important than average tax rates because they are what is most relevant to an individual who must choose what course of action to take, whether to take a new job or to work extra. A high marginal tax rate will reduce gains from working harder and make leisure a more attractive proposition; whereas a lower marginal tax rate will boost the net gains from working and make leisure a more expensive choice.

It is usually the case in graduated direct taxation systems that people's average tax rates are lower than their marginal tax rates. Someone in the UK who makes £50,000 a year will face marginal tax and national insurance contributions (NIC) rate of 41%, which means that he stands to keep only £59 out of every extra £100 he earns (assuming he doesn't use any of the available methods for cutting his tax burden, such as the use of tax-favoured investments such as pensions, and that he doesn't qualify for tax credits). In addition to the marginal hit from the tax and NIC system, this person may also be hit by a reduction in means-tested benefits which could push his marginal tax rate to more than 41%.

By contrast, the average direct tax rate of someone on £50,000 a year will be significantly lower than 41%, because large parts of his income will have been taxed at lower rates or enjoyed zero tax as part of his personal allowance. It is the marginal tax rate faced by an individual that does the most damage by discouraging effort. The average tax rate matters too, but not as much – an individual may look at his average tax burden before deciding to relocate to a jurisdiction with a lower overall tax burden, for example, but on a day to day basis marginal tax rates matter the most.

At the heart of the case for the flat tax is the idea that if the marginal tax rate is brought much closer to the average tax rate, the cost of the tax system will be significantly lower for any given level of revenues raised by taxation. A second is that cutting marginal tax rates almost never reduces tax revenues by as much as the government expects. What should matter from the Exchequer's perspective is the overall amount of revenue generated, and that what counts for revenue generation is average, not marginal tax rates, the case for taking marginal rates down to average rates and to introduce a flat tax is overwhelming.

Lord (Lionel) Robbins, a former director of the London School of Economics and an eminent economist during the 1930s, proposed calculating an "incentive index" to measure the damage created by a tax system. The index is worked out as the ratio between the average and the marginal rates of tax; the idea is that the ratio must be as low as possible to maximise incentives in the economy. If the top rate is 41% and the average rate 18.2%, the ratio is 2.25; however, if both the average and marginal rates were 18.2%, the ratio would be 1; the ratio would be less than 1 if the marginal tax rate is lower than the average tax rate, which is only possible in a regressive tax system. Under a Hall-Rabushka flat tax with a large personal allowance, the ratio would be more than 1 but lower than the current level.

Marginal tax rates in Europe often exceed 50%, while they are less than 40% in most of the US and Japan. As a result, says Goldman Sach's Nielsen, "the tax system provides an important disincentive for European workers to work the odd extra hour or to take an additional part-time job to improve their families' disposable income. As such, the tax system bears part of the blame for the last ten years of lacklustre growth in Continental Europe".[102]

Opponents of lower tax rates or a flat tax make two contrary arguments to try and refute this. The first is that they claim that it is impossible in economic theory to know for sure whether a higher tax will reduce or increase work effort. It is possible, they argue, that a higher tax, by cutting take-home pay, will actually induce people to work harder to compensate for this and to ensure that their living standards do not fall. In this worldview, higher taxes can actually boost economic growth.

In economic jargon, such a model assumes that the income effect of a tax hike outweighs the substitution effect. The latter effect refers to the trade-off between work and leisure; flat-taxers believe that the substitution effect of a higher tax outweighs any income effect, especially for those on high incomes. It is worth remembering that – with the possible exception of some luxury goods, where price becomes a positive attribute in itself – there are no or virtually no known instances of a higher price boosting the demand for a product. So-called Giffen goods appear to be no more than a theoretical curiosity. A higher opportunity cost of leisure ought therefore to be assumed a priori to reduce demand for it and hence boost work.

In the UK, a 13-point reduction in the top tax rate from 41% to 28%, as proposed in the final chapter of this book, would increase the amount of extra earnings kept by a top-rate taxpayer from £59 to £72, a rise of £13 or 22%. The question is: how does taxable income react to this kind of post-tax increase? In economics jargon, the idea is to calculate the elasticity – or responsiveness – of taxable income to changes in after tax income on a marginal pound.

A more restrictive way to look at this is to look at the price elasticity of labour: by how much does the supply of labour increase for a given increase in take-home pay. If the answer were that a 10% rise in after tax earnings were to boost the supply of

102 Nielsen, op. cit.

labour by 10%, the elasticity would be 1; if the 10% were translated into a 5% rise the elasticity would be 0.5. In other words, the elasticity of labour is the increase of the supply of labour divided by the increase in the wage from labour. The elasticities of higher paid workers, older workers and women tend to be higher than average because most workers cannot vary the numbers of hours they work. Numerous studies have found that lower tax rates encourage women to enter the workforce or men to delay partial or full retirement; given that working patterns are becoming more flexible in modern information societies, with greater numbers of people self-employed, the incentive effect of a flat tax ought to be expected to increase over time, strengthening the case yet further. It is also important to realise that the measured number of hours in work is at best an incomplete measure of the work effort: what also matters is the quality of work and the degree of entrepreneurialism it implies.

Some economists have therefore tried to calculate a broader measure called the elasticity of taxable income, which they hope accounts for some of these hard-to-measure effects. Another point worth considering: under high taxes, people may work in jobs with which they are not satisfied; but if the rewards suddenly surge, a reallocation of labour may well take place which may not be measured in standard statistics.

In the UK, Patrick Minford and Paul Ashton found that for top earners, the elasticity of labour was about one, whereas for average earners it was about 0.2.[103] In the US, several top economists have published studies trying to measure the elasticity of labour or of taxable income (a broader concept), some of which are reviewed by Chris Edwards.[104] Lawrence Lindsey found an elasticity greater than one, which means that a 10% boost to after-tax marginal income would boost supply by more than 10%.[105] Other studies have found elasticities as great as 3 (meaning that a 10% increase in post-tax marginal income would boost taxable income by 30%).[106]

More recently, results have been less bullish but have found an elasticity of at least 0.4 with the most responsiveness for people on higher incomes, further buttressing the case for a flat tax.[107]

A review of the microeconomic literature on the subject found the average labour economist believes that the compensated elasticity of labour supply is 0.18 for men and 0.43 for women.[108] By contrast, macroeconomists often find a bigger impact: in his 2004 paper showing that high taxes are the reason why Europeans work less hard

103 Patrick Minford & P Ashton (1989), *The Poverty Trap and the Laffer Curve - What Can the GHS Tell Us?*, CEPR discussion paper no 275, revised December 1989; published in Oxford Economic Papers, 43, 1991, pp. 245-279.
104 Edwards, op. cit.
105 Lawrence Lindsey (1987), *Individual Taxpayer Response to Tax Cuts, 1982-1984, With Implications for the Revenue Maximizing Tax Rate*, Journal of Political Economy (33)
106 Gerald Auten & Robert Carroll (1994), *Taxpayer Behavior and the 1986 Tax Reform Act*, Office of Tax Analysis, U.S. Treasury, July; Feldstein, Martin. 1995. "The Effect of Marginal Tax Rates on Taxable Income: A Panel Study of the 1986 Tax Act," *Journal of Political Economy*, June
107 Gerald Auten & Robert Carroll (1999), *The Effect of Income Taxes on Household Income*, Review of Economics and Statistics 81(4); Gruber, Jonathan and Saez, Emmanuel. 2000. *The Elasticity of Taxable Income: Evidence and Implications*, NBER Working Paper 7512, January
108 'Economists' Views about Parameters, Values, and Policies: Survey Results in Labour and Public Economics', Victor R. Fuchs, Alan B. Krueger & James M. Poterba, *Journal of Economic Literature*, 36(3), September 1998, pp. 1387-1425.

than Americans, 2004 Nobel Prize winner in economics Edward Prescott found on the basis of international comparisons that the compensated elasticity of labour supply is about 3.[109] As usual in economics, there is no consensus on the size of the response to higher taxes – but that there is a response there is no doubt, as the most recent review of the literature highlights. [110]

Economist Donald Bruce has shown that reducing the tax rate an individual expects to face as an entrepreneur increases entrepreneurial activity; however, reducing the tax rate an individual expects to face in a wage job decreases entrepreneurial activity. But the first effect is larger than the second which means that this "suggests that across-the-board tax cuts could increase entrepreneurial start-up and survival".[111]

A series of important papers by Carroll, Holtz-Eakin, Rider, and Rosen have shown that high marginal tax rates reduce the rate at which firms grow their sales, invest and hire.[112] A paper by Gentry and Hubbard[113] has shown that chances of becoming self-employed go up as tax rates become less progressive and that high marginal tax rates reduce successful self-employment.

Gentry and Hubbard have also looked at how tax rates affect whether or not people want to change their jobs.[114] Their paper states: "higher tax rates and increased tax rate progressivity decrease the probability that a head of household will move to a better job during the coming year. Our estimates imply that a five-percentage-point reduction in the marginal tax rate increases the average probability of moving to a better job by 0.79 percentage points (an 8% increase in the turnover propensity) and that a one-standard-deviation decrease in our measure of tax progressivity would increase this probability by 0.86 percentage points (a 8.7% increase in the turnover propensity). Our estimated importance of tax policy for job turnover suggests a potential role in explaining the responsiveness of taxable income to marginal tax rates".

109 'Why Do Americans Work So Much More Than Europeans?', Edward C. Prescott, NBER Working Paper 10316, February 2004: http://minneapolisfed.org/research/qr/qr2811.pdf
110 For a recent review, see Seth H. Giertz, Recent Literature on Taxable-Income Elasticities, Congressional Budget Office, December 2004: http://www.cbo.gov/ftpdocs/60xx/doc6028/2004-16.pdf
111 Donald Bruce, The Effects of Taxes on Entrepreneurial Activity, A Presentation to the President's Advisory Panel on Federal Tax Reform, 8 March 2005: http://www.taxreformpanel.gov/meetings/docs/bruce_03082005.ppt#12 ;also see references therein
112 Robert Carroll, Douglas Holtz-Eakin, Mark Rider & Harvey S. Rosen (2001), Personal Income Taxes and the Growth of Small Firms, in James Poterba (ed), Tax Policy and the Economy, Vol 15, Cambridge, MA: MIT Press; Carroll, Robert, Douglas Holtz-Eakin, Mark Rider, and Harvey S. Rosen (2000) "Entrepreneurs, Income Taxes, and Investment", in Joel B. Slemrod (ed), Does Atlas Shrug? The Economic Consequences of Taxing the Rich, New York: Russell Sage Foundation; Carroll, Robert, Douglas Holtz-Eakin, Mark Rider, and Harvey S. Rosen (2000), "Income Taxes and Entrepreneurs' Use of Labour", Journal of Labour Economics 18(2): 324-351; these papers are also available from the National Bureau of Economic Research.
113 William M. Gentry and R. Glenn Hubbard (2000), Tax Policy and Entrepreneurial Entry, American Economic Review 90(May): 283-287 http://www0.gsb.columbia.edu/faculty/ghubbard/Papers/gentryhubbardtaxpolicyandentryaug2000.pdf
114 William M. Gentry and R. Glenn Hubbard (2004), The effects of progressive income taxation on job turnover, Journal of Public Economics 88, Issue 11 , September 2004, pages 2301-2322

Raising the returns to investment and education

The previous section discussed how a flat tax boosts incentives; it is worth taking a closer look at investment decisions. The latest official figures confirm that businesses remained reluctant to invest in the British economy. The Hall-Rabushka policy of making all capital spending immediately tax-deductible would be bound to boost investment. It makes sense to tax consumption, rather than investment, and this reform would help reverse the collapse in investment suffered by the UK.

It also often forgotten how the current income tax system discourages the accumulation of human capital. The decision to embark on a non-subsidised post-graduate degree such as a Masters in Business Administration (MBA) is always a difficult one; potential students often calculate how much they hope it would increase their income and compare it to the opportunity cost of taking a year or two off work, as well as the fees. If the net present value of an additional degree is not positive, it makes no sense to embark upon it. By reducing the returns to the degree, a graduated income tax system makes it less worthwhile for students to invest in education and hence discourages the accumulation of human capital. Exactly the same sort of reasoning is applicable to other sorts of investment, including traditional capital expenditure. A flat tax would therefore increase the amount of productivity-enhancing education and training in the UK economy.

Economic growth effects of a flat tax

There is plenty of empirical and theoretical evidence that low taxes boost economic growth. However, the fact that the Eastern European flat tax reforms are in the main very recent means that there have so far been few rigorous evaluations of growth effects on those countries. It is also important to note that because none of these countries operates a pure flat tax, any assessment can only be of the actual reform, as opposed to the theoretical Hall-Rabushka model.

Calculations by economist John Chown, based on figures from the European Bank for Reconstruction and Development, reveal that Estonia enjoyed nearly 73% growth over the 10-year period since 1994, against an average of 35% for all transitional economies.[115] Russia has under-performed during this 10-year period; however, its growth since 1998 has been one of the best of the group, in part because of the reforms to its tax code.

Separate research from Goldman Sachs economist Eric Nielsen illustrates that flat tax countries have been extremely successful economically (see figure 6).

115 John Chown (2005), *Flat Taxes: The Case For Radical Tax Reform*, Policy Institute:
http://www.policyinstitute.info/AllPDFs/ChownMay05.pdf

FIGURE 6: BOOST TO GROWTH IN FLAT TAX COUNTRIES

Average GDP Growth Three Years Before and After Introduction of Flat Taxes

	3 Years before	3 Years after
Estonia	-8.4	+6.3
Latvia	-5.0	+5.3
Lithuania	-15.8	+5.1
Russia	+7.2	+6.4
Slovakia	+4.9	+5.5*
Romania	+4.3	+5.0*

* Includes estimates

Source: Goldman Sachs

In a recent paper, think-tank Reform has calculated that since 1995, east European countries with a flat tax have grown twice as fast as those countries without (an annual GDP growth rate of 5.3% compared to 2.6%.[116] The research excludes countries affected by war, including Serbia and Croatia, and those that are still communist dictatorships, such as Belarus.

A similar result can be found by simply comparing last year's economic growth rate with the flat tax rate (see figure 7). The figures should be taken with a pinch of salt as they are from different sources and subject to constant revisions, especially for forecasts. (The avergage calculated is not weighted).

116 Reform Bulletin, 8 September 2005,
http://www.reform.co.uk/website/pressroom/bulletinarchive.aspx?o=110

FIGURE 7: INTERNATIONAL GROWTH RATES

Flat Tax Rates and GDP Growth Rates		
Country	**Flat Tax Rate**	**2004 [2005f]]Growth Rate**
Estonia	24%	7.8% [5.9%]
Georgia	12%	6.2% [8.5%]
Hong Kong	16%	8.2% [5.7%]
Latvia	25%	8.3% [6.7%]
Lithuania	33%	7% [7%]
Romania	16%	8.3% [5%]
Russia	13%	7.4% [5.7%]
Serbia	14%	7.2% [5%]
Slovakia	19%	5.1% [5.4%]
Ukraine	13%	12.1% [3.7%]
Average	18.5%	7.7% [5.9%]

Source: World Bank website; Economist Intelligence Unit; International Monetary Fund; CIA; Ukraine Institute for Economic Research and Policy Consulting; other institutions; author's estimates and calculations

The expected growth rate this year is lower than last, largely because of the global economic slowdown. However, these results showing the strength of flat tax countries – while fascinating – are not conclusive in themselves as they do not control for all other influences. For a start, as we shall see later on, the flat tax rates do not include national insurance contributions, which means that simple comparisons are misleading. More fundamentally, however, to calculate a simple bivariate correlation between one policy – the introduction of flat taxes – and economic growth and to claim that the relationship between the two is unambiguously causal would not be good economics. Chown, Goldman Sachs, and Reform do not make this mistake. But what the correlation they identify does show is that flat taxes – or at least the version introduced in Eastern European countries – do not lead to economic catastrophe, swamping the effect of all other more positive variables.

Tax evasion in Britain

In 1979, Sir William Pile, then chairman of the British Revenue Board, produced the first modern estimate of tax evasion and found that "it was not implausible" that untaxed earnings equalled 7.5% of UK GDP. This led academics to try measuring the underground economy by various methods.[117] The American economist Edgar Feige thought Sir William was half right and put the true figure at closer to 15% of GDP in 1979.

---

117 '*Europe's Underground Economies*', National Center for Policy Analysis: http://www.ncpa.org/ba/ba278.html

There have been several estimates since then. One notable analysis was produced in 1997 by Deloitte, which estimated that the underground economy was worth 12% of UK GDP and reduced income tax revenues by one-third. A review in 2004 of six independent studies found estimates ranging from 5.5% to 13.2%, with an average of 9.3%; under-reporting of incomes is more prevalent among blue-collar workers than those in white-collar jobs. The three authors of the review produce their own estimate at 10.6% of GDP for 2002.[118] In a separate paper published in Norway in April 2005, the size of the UK black economy was estimated at 12.4%.[119]

However, what must surely be the seminal quantification comes in a paper dated June 2005 by Friedrich Schneider, of the Johannes Kepler University of Linz, one of the world's top experts on the shadow economy.[120] Schneider argues that the average size of the shadow economy as a percent of "official" GDP in 2002-03 in 96 developing countries was 38.7%, in 25 transition countries 40.1%, in 21 OECD countries 16.3% and in 3 Communist countries 22.3%. In Britain, it is now 12.2% of GDP, Schneider believes. Assuming the share has remained the same since then, on current levels of GDP of £1.16 trillion, the amount of legal activities underreported to HMRC in 2005 would be around £141.5bn. By contrast, the share in the US is a mere 8.4% but in France it is 14.5% and in Germany 16.8%.

Crucially, criminal activities are not included in Schneider's research. He defines the shadow economy as all market-based legal production of goods and services that are deliberately concealed from public authorities to avoid paying income, value added or other taxes or national insurance contributions; to avoid having to meet certain legal labour market standards, such as minimum wages, maximum working hours, safety standards; and to avoid the other kinds of red tape with which the official economy is burdened, such as legal requirements to fill in statistical questionnaires. There are two ways of estimating the size of the black economy. The first is the direct approach and relies on polls and surveys and examining the result of spot tax-audits. This method doesn't work very well. People tend not to be honest when replying to surveys and the findings from the government's spot audits are not representative of what is happening in the economy as a whole.

The second, indirect method, is much more effective. It is based on studying the evolution over time of cash transactions, electricity consumption or other proxies for economic activity or trade, and comparing these with official figures. If the rate at which money is being used in the economy is going up faster than the rate of economic growth, ceteris paribus, this would suggest that the black economy is growing.

118 'Estimates of the Black Economy Based on Consumer Demand Approaches', P. Lyssiotou, P. Pashardes, & T. Stengos, *Economic Journal*, July 2004, pp. 622-640.
119 Knut R. Wangen, *An Expenditure Based Estimate of Britain's Black Economy Revisited*, Discussion Papers No. 414, April 2005, Statistics Norway, Research Department: http://www.ssb.no/publikasjoner/DP/pdf/dp414.pdf
120 Friedrich Schneider (2005), *Shadow Economies of 145 Countries all over the World: What Do We Really Know?*, Center for Research in Economics, Management and the Arts: http://www.crema-research.ch/papers/2005-13.pdf

What makes Schneider's research especially interesting is that he examines the reasons why the size of underground economies varies over time and between different countries. "An increased burden of taxation and social security contributions, combined with labour market regulation are the driving forces of the shadow economy", Schneider argues.[121]

Schneider sums up thus: "The tax and social security payment burden are the driving forces of the shadow economy closely followed by the status of the official economy for the developed and transition countries and by the tax moral variable for the highly developed OECD countries. For the developing countries the burden of state regulation is the single most important factor". Clearly, therefore, a flat tax and a reduced overall tax burden would reduce the size of the underground economy in Britain, expanding the Treasury's tax base and allowing for lower tax rates.

Even Brown's officials have conceded in writing that the complexity of the case has boosted tax evasion. The Treasury admits that "the lack of credits and exemptions in a flat tax structure should lead to a significant reduction in avoidance and evasion as potential loopholes are eliminated. Furthermore, the reduced ability to evade the tax structure broadens the tax base as grey economies are encouraged to join the open economy. The subsequent increase in compliance therefore results in an overall increase in tax revenue yielded."[122]

Competing against tax havens

The previous section outlined how high tax rates stimulate tax evasion; but another reason why high taxes do not generate as much revenue for the exchequer as Brown would like is legal tax avoidance through so-called tax havens. It is very difficult to estimate the amount and value of assets held in tax havens, or the rate at which this industry is growing, but there can be no doubt that huge amounts of money are being chased away from the UK by our excessively high tax rates. An important appeal of a flat tax and lower taxation in general is to ensure that more of this money stays or comes to Britain. Tax havens have done the world a great service: by exposing rich, over-taxed nations to tax competition, they have been forcing them to cut their taxes – reforms which they should be doing anyway because low taxes are good for growth even in closed economies in a hypothetical non-globalised world.

There are no reliable statistics on how much money there would be for flat tax countries to grab. The problem is that most estimates of the value of assets currently in tax havens are made by groups or organisations that see tax havens as an evil to be fought, rather than an essential escape hatch for overburdened taxpayers.

America's Internal Revenue Service says on its website that "it has been estimated that some $5 trillion in assets worldwide is held 'offshore' in tax havens".[123]

121 Schneider, op. cit.
122 HM Treasury, op. cit
123 *Abusive Offshore Tax Avoidance Schemes* – Talking Points, IRS.gov: http://www.irs.gov/businesses/small/article/0,,id=106568,00.html

A figure that is often mentioned by left-wing groups (and which is based on various sources and estimates) is that tax havens – between 40 and 70 countries, depending on estimates – with no more than 1% of the world's population account for 31% of world assets. It is also sometimes claimed that up to 3m companies have been set up to reduce taxes.[124]

In 2000, a paper from the International Monetary Fund[125] claimed that on-balance sheet offshore-financial centres' cross-border assets reached a level of $4.6 trillion at end-June 1999 (then worth about 50% of total cross-border assets), of which $0.9 trillion was in the Caribbean, $1 trillion in Asia, and most of the remaining US$2.7 trillion accounted for by the International Financial Centers, namely London, the US International Banking Facilities (IBFs) and the Japanese Offshore Market (JOM).

The Tax Justice Network, a radical left-wing group, claims on the basis of extrapolations from data from the Bank for International Settlements (BIS), the 'World Wealth Report', from Merrill Lynch and Cap Gemini and other organisations that the value of assets held offshore lies in the range of $11 - $12 trillion, yielding a return of about US$860bn a year. While this probably exaggerates the size of tax havens, it remains the case that they have captured a large market share of global wealth – and Britain and other Western countries should fight back by cutting their own taxes, not by criticising economies with more competitive tax systems.

A sufficiently low flat tax would eliminate at the stroke of a pen the main advantage for wealthy individuals to send their money to overseas tax havens. It would make Britain's wealthiest entrepreneurs less likely to want to live in foreign tax havens such as Monaco and to engage in tax avoidance. Often, tax exiles would love nothing more than not to leave the UK, but are not prepared to face the cost. Although good weather is a side-benefit, it seems likely that most would spend a much greater part of the year in the UK if their taxes were not as high. For these people, paying 41% tax on their income is not acceptable; however, significantly less would be tolerable. There are always costs as well as benefits to reducing taxes through the use of overseas accounts, tax havens and the tax avoidance industry; cutting the benefits while leaving the costs unchanged would change the calculus for many people. It is the best interests of a country to retain as many of its richest, brightest and most talented business people, entrepreneurs, authors and entertainers – just as it is to attract the monied foreign elites.

Attracting people and capital

The level of taxation is an influential factor for 80% of companies in determining international investment location decisions, according to a CBI/MORI survey on 'The UK

124 'Secretly, tiny nations hold much wealth', David R. Francis, *Christian Science Monitor*.
    http://www.csmonitor.com/2005/0425/p17s01-cogn.html
125 'Offshore Financial Centers', International Monetary Fund Monetary and Exchange Affairs Department, 2000, *IMF.org*.
    http://www.imf.org/external/np/mae/oshore/2000/eng/back.htm#II_B

as a place to do business' in November 2003.[126]

The cost of business taxation determines the returns required for investment decisions to be viable, the level of personal taxation determines the attractiveness of the UK for world-class talent, and tax complexity can add to businesses' compliance costs and affect certainty and confidence.

While Britain is still doing relatively well in the foreign direct investment stakes, it could and should do better with a flat tax. At present, the biggest inflow of funds comes from mergers and acquisitions, rather than ordinary capital projects.

There is increasing evidence that tax rates are important in attracting foreign direct investment. Jeffrey Owens, director of the OECD's centre for tax policy and administration, said: "Empirical evidence is beginning to emerge showing that manufacturing FDI is becoming increasingly geographically mobile and sensitive to host country taxation...This should not surprise us given that many non-tax considerations have become more uniform across countries and therefore have less of an influence on business location."[127]

The latest foreign direct investment (FDI) figures from the UN show that the new EU member states are doing much better than old Europe, and this must partly be to do with their much lower tax rates. The figures reveal that FDI in Central and Eastern Europe jumped 70% in 2004, while FDI in the EU as a whole collapsed 36% to $216bn. In the original 15 EU member states, FDI fell 40% to $196bn, its weakest level since 1998.[128] While Britain has kept its own, this was driven by mergers and acquisitions rather than capital spending. The UK's commitment to free trade and the very high levels of profitability of British industry, caused largely by cyclical effects, explain the large flows of FDI into the country. There is no doubt that under a flat tax Britain would do considerably better.

Until now, research on the effect of tax rates on highly skilled migration had been sorely lacking. However, a new OECD paper has shown overwhelming evidence that lower taxes rates also help attract skilled migrants.[129] Expected wages and job opportunities, the costs of migration, network effects and the subjective evaluation of a location help but the expected net return from migration has also a lot to do with taxation.

Because Swiss tax rates are primarily determined at the local level and thus enough variation exists to analyse their influence on migration, the researchers decided to use Switzerland as a case study for their research. The OECD document states:

"The regression analysis first studies internal migration within Switzerland. ...Clearly, there is a positive relation between the tax differential and the

126 'The CBI Business Agenda', Confederation of British Industry, 2005, http://www.cbi.org.uk/pdf/businessagenda05.pdf
127 Quoted in 'Simpler, lower, fairer: Brown's tax demand from business', Vanessa Houlder, *Financial Times*, 3 October 2005
128 United Nations (2005), *World Investment Report 2005*: http://www.unctad.org/en/docs/wir2005_en.pdf
129 Thomas Liebig and Alfonso Sousa-Poza (2005), *Taxation, Ethnic Ties and the Location Choice of Highly Skilled Immigrants*, working paper: http://www.oecd.org/dataoecd/5/60/35239536.pdf

migration probability. The effect is even stronger for highly qualified people, who are apparently more attracted towards low-tax communities. ...A very robust influence of the tax burden on the share of the highly skilled among the new immigrants can be observed. Indeed, apart from the tax burden, there is little else that is statistically significant... The most important finding of this study is that the community tax burden has a significant impact on highly skilled migration. Both highly skilled natives and immigrants react to tax differences in a similar way, i.e. they are more inclined to migrate to low-tax areas. This result is very robust and holds even after several factors, including qualify-of-life measures, are controlled for."

Dynamic effects

The boost to economic growth and to incomes is the key dynamic effect of moving to a flat tax; it is the reason why tax reform ends up delivering more for less. Lower tax rates lead to faster economic growth and increased asset values; as a result, much and occasionally all of the revenue 'lost' to the government from tax cuts – such a phrase, which is often used by government officials, implies that the money was the state's in the first place, which is nonsense – is recouped. Tax revenues are reduced by less than expected in the months immediately following a tax cut; in the long run they go up, usually at the same rate as economic growth. As economist Arthur Laffer famously put it: too much tax kills tax revenues.

His Laffer Curve, was famously sketched in the late 1970s (see figure 8). This shows how for each level of tax revenues there are two possible tax rates: a low rate and a high rate. A tax rate of 0% and 100% yield the same level of revenues, namely zero. There two possible tax rates for every other level of tax revenues. Unfortunately, unlike with the zero-revenue cases, nobody knows what those rates are. The only exception to this rule is t*, which is the only tax rate that maximises revenues.

FIGURE 8: THE LAFFER CURVE

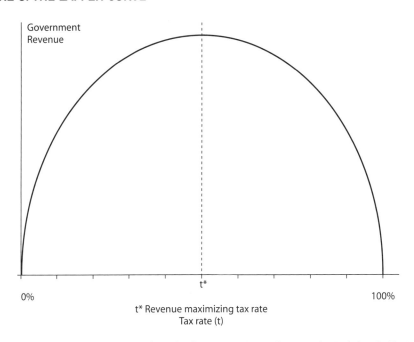

t* Revenue maximizing tax rate

Tax rate (t)

Critics claim that even though flat taxes have been adopted by 9 Eastern European countries, to do so would be unaffordable in Britain. The most important error made by opponents of the flat tax is to forget or refuse to factor in how lower taxes will change people's behaviour, as well as the other Laffer effects. This is the mistake made by almost every opponent of the flat tax.

Claims that a flat tax would lead to a black hole in the Treasury's accounts of £50bn or more are wide off the mark; as is the view that a flat tax would have to make between 10m and 30m worse off. As we shall see in later Chapters of this book, these forecasts are based on arithmetically accurate but economically naïve calculations because they assume that the overall size of the economy and total personal income remains the same regardless of the tax code that is in place. But as we have seen, there is a mass of academic research which shows that lower tax leads to faster economic growth; helps to attract foreign direct investment and capital; and leads to a reduction in tax avoidance.

Unfortunately, groups such as the Institute for Fiscal Studies have failed to include such dynamic effects in their models[130]; as a result, they dramatically over-estimate the reduction in tax revenues that would accompany a flat tax. A proper economic model would show that tax revenues are reduced by less than expected in the short term following a cut in the top rate of income tax; in the long run they would go

---

130 See the model at http://www.bized.ac.uk/virtual/economy/model/Hard.html

up, usually at the same rate as economic growth. There are only two supply-side models of the UK economy: that developed by David Smith, chief economist at Williams de Broe, which responds to the tax to GDP ratio but because of a lack of resources isn't able to quantify the impact of a change in marginal tax rates; and the Liverpool Macroeconomic Research model, developed by Patrick Minford (some of its findings are described later in this book).

There is a similar problem with official government models in the US but at least there a vigorous campaign is being waged by a coalition of more than 40 free-market think-tanks to remedy it. In a recent letter, they asked (with little success, sadly) President Bush to tell his Advisory Panel on Federal Tax Reform to adopt 'reality-based' revenue estimating methodology. The panel chose to stick to static revenue estimating techniques. But these estimates assume that tax policy changes - regardless of their magnitude - have no impact on the economy's performance and thus overstate both the amount of tax revenue that will be generated by tax increases and the amount of revenue the government will 'lose' because of tax rate cuts. This 'static' methodology provides policy makers with inaccurate numbers and creates a bias against lower tax rates, the groups are rightly arguing. Dynamic analysis – sometimes referred to as 'reality-based scoring' or 'dynamic scoring' – acknowledges that taxes do affect the economy through its supply-side and that higher tax rates discourage work, saving, and investment, and therefore will not raise as much revenues as the static estimates would suggest.[131]

How cutting tax has boosted revenues worldwide

As well as boosting growth, a flat tax would make it less worthwhile for people to hide their income from the taxman. This would reduce the size of Britain's underground economy. Many people who are currently already paying the top rate of tax would enjoy very strong increases in income and also pay more tax, even if a smaller proportion of their income. Britain's wealthiest entrepreneurs would be less likely to want to live in foreign tax havens such as Monaco.

In Russia, income tax revenues increased by 25.2% in real terms for the fiscal year after introducing its flat rate in 2001, by 24.6% in 2002, by 15.2% in 2003 and by 14.4% in 2004. The IMF estimates that there was a 16% increase in the proportion of income declared, partly due to improved enforcement.[132]

For those who believe that the lessons of post-communist Eastern Europe cannot apply to the UK, there is plenty of evidence from the US.[133] There have been four major rounds of tax cuts in recent US history and they have all led to positive supply-side effects and higher tax receipts. The Revenue Acts of 1921, 1924, and 1926 slashed the

131 For the letter to the president see http://www.freedomandprosperity.org/ltr/president2/president2.shtml
132 See Rabushka's papers on http://www.russianeconomy.org/comments.html
133 'Research – Taxes', Daniel J. Mitchell, Heritage Foundation: http://www.heritage.org/Research/Taxes/BG1443.cfm

top rate of tax from 73% to 25%. Partly as a result, the US economy boomed. Income tax receipts followed suit: they surged by more than 61% between 1921 and 1928 at a time of zero inflation. There was a similar response when the top rate was reduced from 91% in 1963 to 70% in 1965: the economy grew extremely strongly and tax revenues surged by 62% between 1961 and 1968 (and one-third in real times, according to Daniel J. Mitchell of the Heritage Foundation). President Reagan cut the top tax rate from 70% in 1980 to 28% by 1988. The US economy received its first proper tax cut at the start of 1983. Income tax revenues soon climbed dramatically, increasing by more than 54% by 1989 (28% after adjusting for inflation). Finally, President Bush's tax cuts, while not as radical, did include important supply-side elements, including a reduction in the top tax rate to 35% and a halving of the tax on dividends. The result has yet again been a surge in revenues. Despite predictions of disaster, receipts in the 2005 financial year jumped 14.6% year on year, the highest increase in receipts in over 20 years.[134] Despite surging spending, the 2005 unified deficit was $319bn, or an estimated 2.6% of Gross Domestic Product (GDP). As a percent of GDP, the 2005 deficit was lower than the deficits of 16 of the last 25 years. The surge in tax revenues was led by corporation taxes, which rose from $189.3bn to $278.3bn. Even the budget deficit is down dramatically; it could easily have been eliminated completely a long time ago had President Bush not succumbed to the folly of big government conservatism and gone on a Gordon Brown-style spending binge.

Most recently, another tax-cut 'miracle' has been witnessed in Australia: the amount of tax paid by Australian businesses has surged to record levels despite (or because of) a cut in the company tax rate four years ago. Since 2002-03, company tax payments have surged from just under A$33bn to A$50bn. Payments by the self-employed and investors have risen by 40% to A$22.5bn over the past three years. The company tax rate was cut to 30% from 36% as a result of recent tax reforms.[135]

Most astonishing of all is what has happened to Irish company tax revenues since tax rates were cut. According to research by top economists Eric Engen and Kevin Hassett, in the mid-1980s, when Ireland's corporate income tax rate was close to 50%, it raised just more than 1% of Ireland's GDP in tax revenues. However, today's 12.5% corporate tax raises revenue totaling nearly 4% of GDP[136]. The case of Ireland's company taxes is a clear illustration of pure Laffer-style effects. Not only did the massive tax rate cuts not lead to reductions in tax revenue, either in cash terms or as a share of GDP, they actually went hand in hand with an explosion in tax revenues. It is astonishing that this incredible success story is almost never talked about in the UK.

---

134 Budget Results, 2005 fiscal year, US Treasury: http://www.ustreas.gov/press/releases/reports/yes05combinedfinal.pdf
135 'Australian Company Tax Take Jumps Despite Rate Cuts', Mary Swire, *Tax-News.com*, 12 September 2005:
   http://www.tax-news.com/asp/story/story_open.asp?storyname=21078
136 Eric Engen and Kevin Hassett (2003), *Does the U.S. Corporate Tax Have a Future?*, Tax Notes, Spring 2003:
   http://www.aei.org/docLib/20021222_raengehass0212.pdf

FIGURE 9: CORPORATE TAX RATE AND REVENUE IN IRELAND

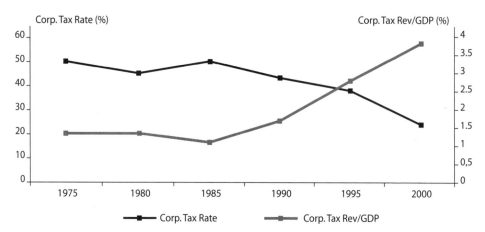

Source: Eric Engen and Kevin Hassett, "Does the Corporate Tax Have a Future?" Tax Notes, Spring 2003, at http://www.aei.org/docLib/20021222_raengehass0212.pdf

As the Economist Intelligence Unit points out, there is no evidence from across the OECD that big tax cuts undermine receipts[137]. It also highlights the case of Ireland, which cleverly introduced the lowest company tax rate (at 12.5%) in the EU-15 – it remains in second position even when the new members are included – and which collected 13% of its total tax receipts in corporation tax in 2002. In stark contrast, Germany, with a high headline corporate tax rate, raised a mere 0.6% of GDP from corporate tax receipts, 1.5% of its total. It is an unimpeachable fact that most OECD member states reduced their corporate tax rates in the 1980s and 1990s, but corporate tax receipts remained broadly stable as a share of GDP during that time[138].

In an analysis of the Bush tax cuts, economist Martin Feldstein predicted that it would produce a dynamic feedback effect of at least 25% or $400bn of the static revenue change of $1.6 trillion.[139] The Heritage Foundation calculated that 2001 tax cuts would produce dynamic revenue feedbacks worth 47% of the 10-year static revenue reduction.[140] Larry Lindsey calculated in a 1987 paper that supply-side effects compensated for up to a quarter of the 1981 tax cut. Robert Carroll estimated that the US tax hike of 1993 marginal tax rate suffered from the fact that supply-side effects cut the static revenue gain by between 13% and 39%.[141]

In a recent paper which tries to assess the extent to which a tax cut pays for

137 'Romania economy: Will the tax changes fall flat?', Economist Intelligence Unit, 13 January 2005,
    http://www.viewswire.com/index.asp?layout=display_print&doc_id=1387942138
138 Economist Intelligence Unit, op. cit
139 'The 28% Solution', Martin Feldstein, Wall Street Journal, 16 February 2001
140 'The Economic and Budgetary Effects of President Bush's Tax Relief Plan', Mark Wilson and William Beach, The Heritage Foundation,
    22 February 2001, http://www.heritage.org/Research/Taxes/CDA01-01.cfm
141 Robert Carroll, Do Taxpayers Really Respond to Changes in Tax Rates? Evidence from the 1993 Tax Act, OTA Working Paper 79,
    U.S. Treasury Department. November 1998, http://www.treas.gov/ota/ota79.pdf

itself through higher economic growth, Gregory Mankiw and Matthew Weinzierl, prominent Harvard economists, wrote:

> *"In all of the models considered here, the dynamic response of the economy to tax changes is too large to be ignored. In almost all cases, tax cuts are partly self-financing. This is especially true for cuts in capital income taxes. Not surprisingly, the results of this exercise depend on a number of key parameters. Because the values of some of these parameters are open to debate, reasonable people can disagree about the magnitude of the feedback effects. Two crucial parameters are the compensated elasticity of labour supply and the externality to capital accumulation. Unfortunately, the empirical literature does not give clear guidance about their magnitudes. The degree of imperfect competition may also be important, but only to the extent that market power leads to pure economic profits."* [142]

For the parameter values used by Mankiw and Weinzierl, which they themselves acknowledge are uncertain, they find that the steady-state feedback of a capital tax cut is 50% and that of a labour tax cut is 16.7% — in other words, that a capital tax cut reduces revenues by half the amount forecast by static models. Assuming greater elasticities would mean that tax cuts would reduce revenues by even less; some economists go significantly further than Mankiw and Weinzierl.

The conclusion of any serious economic research must therefore be that dynamic and static revenue estimation can lead to very different results. The fact that the UK Treasury as well as independent research organisations such as the Institute for Fiscal Studies do not try to estimate the dynamic, supply-side feedback effects of tax cuts is a major problem for UK public policy making. It means that all discussions of public policy have an inherent bias towards the status quo and against tax cuts because they will always exaggerate their effects on revenues. This is especially problematic with the Treasury's so-called ready-reckoners[143], which have helped propagate an erroneous static view of the UK economy.

High tax wedge between labour cost and take-home pay

A flat tax would also be good for jobs if it reduces the tax on labour and the so-called tax wedge. The tax wedge is the difference between the total labour cost and wage costs – in other words it measures non-wage costs such as national insurance contributions that employers have to pay in addition to wages.

---

142 *'Dynamic Scoring: A Back-of-the-Envelope Guide'*, N. Gregory Mankiw & Matthew Weinzierl, Harvard University, 7 April 2005:
  http://post.economics.harvard.edu/hier/2005papers/HIER2057.pdf
143 HM Treasury, Tax Ready Reckoners and Tax Relief, December 2004,
  http://www.hm-treasury.gov.uk/media/8F5/9F/pbr04tax_ready_182.pdf

High tax wedges are bad for economic efficiency and jobs. According to a basic regression run by ING (see figure 10), higher tax wedges are accompanied by higher unemployment rates. Obviously, this sort of statistical analysis is not rigorous because it doesn't control for the myriad other factors that influence employment and unemployment levels, such as red tape and economic growth. But it does nevertheless serve a useful illustrative purpose.

FIGURE 10: TAX WEDGES AND UNEMPLOYMENT

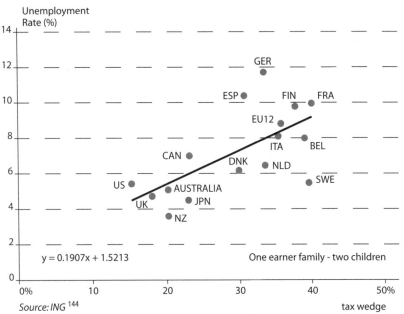

Source: ING [144]

In most OECD countries, employers pay significant social security contributions.[145] In 2004, according to an OECD report on the subject, the tax wedge between total labour costs to the employer and the corresponding net take-home pay to single workers without children, at average earnings levels, varied widely (see figure 11). The tax wedge exceeded 50% in Belgium and Germany and was lower than 20% in Korea and Mexico.

The share of labour costs from personal income tax is less than 5% in Greece, Korea, Mexico and Portugal and exceeds 30% in Denmark; that made up by employee social security ranges from 0% in Australia, Iceland and New Zealand to over 20% in the Netherlands and Poland. Employers pay 28.2% total labour costs in social security contributions in France, 26.9% in Hungary, 26.3% in the Slovak Republic, and 25.9% in the Czech Republic; they pay nothing in New Zealand and virtually nothing in Denmark.

144 The Wrath of God, *Global Economics*, September 2005, ING
145 OECD, Taxing Wages 2003-04
    http://www.oecd.org/document/49/0,2340,en_2649_34533_30481201_1_1_1_1,00.html
    and also Taxing Wages 2003-04, 2004 Edition, OECD

FIGURE 11: INCOME TAX AND SOCIAL SECURITY CONTRIBUTIONS
(% of Labour costs), 2004 [1]

Country (2)	Income tax %	Social security contributions		Total (3) %	Labour costs (4) $
		employee %	employer %		
Belgium	20.5	10.7	23.0	54.2	46,261
Germany	16.2	17.3	17.3	50.7	42,543
Australia	22.9	0.0	5.7	28.6	40,630
Netherlands	7.3	22.2	14.0	43.6	39,614
Switzerland	8.9	10.0	10.0	28.8	38,213
Canada	16.0	6.2	10.1	32.3	37.856
Denmark	30.4	10.5	0.5	41.5	37,788
United States	15.4	7.1	7.1	29.6	37,606
Norway	18.5	6.9	11.5	36.9	37,550
Finland	19.5	4.9	19.4	43.8	37,174
United Kingdom	14.5	7.8	9.0	31.2	36,159
Korea	2.0	6.5	8.1	16.6	36,125
Luxembourg	7.9	12.1	11.9	31.9	35,767
France	9.4	9.8	28.2	47.4	35,443
Japan	5.2	10.3	11.1	26.6	35,103
Italy	14.0	6.9	24.9	45.7	35,005
Sweden	18.1	5.3	24.6	48.0	34,606
Austria	8.4	14.0	22.5	44.9	34,356
Iceland	24.1	0.2	5.4	29.7	32,194
Ireland	9.6	4.5	9.7	23.8	30,236
Spain	9.7	4.9	23.4	38.0	29,382
New Zealand	20.7	0.0	0.0	20.7	28,228
Greece	0.5	12.5	21.9	34.9	22,138
Turkey	12.7	12.3	17.7	42.7	20,007
Czech Republic	8.4	9.3	25.9	43.6	19,395
Poland	5.1	21.1	17.0	43.1	17,319
Portugal	4.5	8.9	19.2	32.6	16,128
Slovak Republic	5.8	9.9	26.3	42.0	13,997
Hungary	9.0	9.9	26.9	45.8	13,229
Mexico	2.6	1.3	11.4	15.4	10,278

1. Single individual without children at the income level of the average production worker.
2. Countries ranked by decreasing labour costs.
3. Due to rounding total may differ one percentage point from aggregate of columns for income tax and social security contributions.
4. Dollars with equal purchasing power.

Source: OECD: http://www.oecd.org/dataoecd/33/28/34545117.pdf

Cutting taxes for the poor

It is an astonishing fact that in today's Britain, the poor pay a greater proportion of their income in taxes than those on the highest incomes. This was confirmed yet again by the most recent evidence, released in July 2005 by the Office for National Statistics but dating back to the 2003-04 financial year.[146]

One problem is that there are now 30.5m income taxpayers, far more than the 23m seen in 1973-74 and under 4m in 1938-9, when income tax only hit the better off. Under Chancellor Gordon Brown, income-tax payers numbers have surged from 26.2m to 30.5m; the number of top-rate taxpayers has gone up at an even faster rate from 2.1m to 3.6m.

Another problem is that, as the Liberal Democrats put it in their consultation paper: "The UK tax system is not progressive… Direct taxation is progressive … but indirect taxes counterbalance this. All the major indirect taxes are regressive, the most strikingly so being tobacco duty which accounts for ten times as much of the income of the bottom 20% of households as of the top 20%".[147]

However, these figures do not take into account the effect of tax credits. Taking into account all benefits as well as taxes and tax credits, the net effect of government fiscal policy is to substantially narrow the gap between original incomes and final incomes – but the point here is to look only at the tax system, not welfare benefits, which is what tax credits really are.

The analysis which follows treats all tax credits as welfare payments and not as negative taxation, which is the right way to proceed. The definition of income used is gross income (which is original income plus cash benefits, different from the definition used in Figure 25 Chapter IX). The total tax burden on the bottom 20% of the population ranked by household income is a staggering 38%. For the next quintile up, this falls to 33.6%; the third quintile pays 35.8%; the fourth quintile 36.7%; and the top 20% fork out 35.5%. The average for all households is 35.8%. Every quintile pays less tax than the poorest 20%.

146 The effect of taxes and benefits on household income, 2003-04,
    http://www.statistics.gov.uk/articles/nojournal/taxesbenefits200304/taxesbenefits200304.pdf
147 Liberal Democrat Federal Policy Committee (2005), Federal Policy Consultation Paper No. 78
    http://www.libdems.org.uk/media/documents/policies/78%20Tax.pdf

FIGURE 12: A REGRESSIVE TAX SYSTEM

Direct and indirect taxes as a percentage of gross income, disposable income and expenditure for all households by quintile groups, with tax credits treated wholly as a benefit, 2003-04

Percentages of gross income	Quintile groups of all households					All households
	Bottom	2nd	3rd	4th	Top	
Direct taxes						
Income tax	3.8	7.2	10.7	13.9	18.4	13.9
Employees' NIC	1.4	2.8	4.4	5.3	4.6	4.3
Council tax & Northern Ireland rates	4.9	3.6	3.0	2.5	1.7	2.5
All direct taxes	10.1	13.6	18.2	21.7	24.6	20.7
Indirect taxes						
VAT	10.6	8.0	7.3	6.3	4.9	6.3
Duty on Alcohol	1.5	1.2	1.1	0.9	0.6	0.9
Duty on Tabacco	3.2	1.8	1.3	0.9	0.4	1.0
Duty on hydrocarbon oils & Vehicle exercise duty	2.9	2.4	2.3	2.1	1.4	1.9
Other indirect taxes	9.6	6.6	5.6	4.8	3.6	4.9
All Indirect taxes	27.9	20.0	17.6	15.0	10.9	15.1
All taxes	38.0	33.6	35.8	36.7	35.5	35.8

Source: Office for National Statistics, The effect of taxes and benefits on household income, from Table 3A op. cit.

This would change under a flat tax as proposed in the final Chapter of this book. The poor would no longer have to pay income tax and national insurance contributions; they would still pay indirect taxes which hit all households but their situation would be significantly improved.

At present, the bottom quintile pays 3.8% of its income in income tax and 1.4% in employee national insurance contributions; adding in council tax and Northern Ireland rates takes the direct tax take to 10.1% of their gross incomes. The second quintile pays 7.2% of its income in income tax and 2.8% in employee national insurance contributions.

The share of the better off would also fall. But whenever top tax rates have been cut in the past, in the UK as well as the US and other countries, the share of the total tax burden paid by the better-off has always increased. This is because they are encouraged to use their talents and energy and tend to enjoy huge increases in income, and hence pay more tax despite the lower tax rate. They are also much less likely to avoid tax as it becomes less worthwhile to employ expensive tax advisers.

It makes no sense for the poor (or the middle classes, for that matter) to pay taxes and then much or all of their money back in benefits. This financial "churn" is very wasteful, both in terms of incentives (taxes make it less worthwhile to work, benefits trap people on welfare) and also because a large chunk of the money is siphoned off in costs and wages of public sector workers. It would make much more sense for the poor to pay no direct taxes – and perhaps to be given fewer benefits. The same is true for the better off: it is ridiculous for them to pay huge amounts of tax and then to get much of it back through the welfare state.

FIGURE 13: UK TAX AND BENEFITS

Income, taxes and benefits per household (£ per year)	Quintile groups of all households						Ratio
	Bottom £	2nd £	3rd £	4th £	Top £	All households	Top/Bottom quintile
Original income	3,750	10,410	20,710	32,630	63,150	26,130	17
plus cash benefits	5,910	6,090	4,360	2,690	1,420	4,100	0
Gross income	9,660	16,500	25,070	35,330	64,570	30,230	7
less direct taxes and employees' NIC	930	2,050	4,380	7,540	15,890	6,160	17
Disposable income	8,730	14,450	20,700	27,780	48,680	24,070	6
less indirect taxes	2,710	3,350	4,460	5,320	7,030	4,570	3
Post-tax income	6,020	11,100	16,240	22,460	41,650	19,500	7
plus benefits in kind	5,720	5,280	5,020	4,270	3,340	4,730	1
Final income	11,750	16,380	21,270	26,730	44,990	24,220	4

Source: Office for National Statistics, The effect of taxes and benefits on household income, from Table 4, op. cit.: authors' calculations.

The bottom 20% of households receive £5,910 in cash benefits and £5,720 in benefits in kind, a total of £11,630. But they pay £930 in direct taxes and £2,710 in indirect taxes, or £3,640. The welfare state makes them better off by £7,990.

The second quartile receive cash benefits of £6,090 and benefits in kind of £5,280, a total of £11,370. They pay direct tax of £2,050 and indirect taxes of £3,350, a total of £5,400. The welfare state makes them better off by £5,970.

The third quartile receives cash benefits of £4,360 and benefits in kind of £5,020, a total of £9,380. They pay direct tax of £4,380 and indirect tax of £4,460, a total of £8,840. The welfare state makes them better off by £540.

The fourth quartile receive cash benefits of £2,690 and benefits in kind of £4,270, a total of £6,960. They pay direct taxes of £7,540 and indirect taxes of £5,320, a total of £12,860. The welfare state makes them worse off by £5,900.

The top 20% of households receive cash benefits of £1,420 and benefits in kind worth £3,340, a total of £4,760. They pay £15,890 in direct taxes and £7,030 in indirect taxes

– summing to a massive £22,920. The welfare state makes them worse off by £18,160.

These are some of the most remarkable statistics available about the British welfare state. They suggest that in the aggregate, all sections of the population could afford cuts in spending as long as these are matched by cuts in direct taxes. In the case of the wealthier half or so of the population, all cash and non-cash benefits could be terminated, matched by huge reductions in taxes, and they would in the aggregate not be any worse off. The aim of any rational tax policy – such as the proposal for a UK flat tax developed in this book – should be to reduce the churn of taxing people on the one hand and giving them money back on the other. This causes dead-weight costs, reduced incentives and wastage.

Tax Credits in Crisis

One of the innovations Chancellor Gordon Brown is most proud of since he took office in 1997 is his embrace of tax credits as a way to deliver targeted benefits to relatively poor families with children and lower income people in work. Tax credits use the income tax system, rather than the more traditional welfare route, to deliver benefits.

Under the present system, 3.6m people who earn half of average earnings nevertheless still pay income tax. Instead of taking these people out of the direct tax system, Brown's answer has been to introduce ever more complex tax credits to help his favourite groups, namely families with children and those in work. The result has been an administrative nightmare. Not only is the system far too complicated for most families to grasp, it is also constructed in such a way as to make over-payments and errors inevitable, with past income triggering payments – even though current income is what determines entitlements.

In June 2005, two reports revealed that the tax credit scheme is in crisis, with millions of families being under or overpaid. The system is meant to help low income families, but the Citizen's Advice Bureau pointed out that it has "plunged many below the breadline and into mounting debt"[148]. Meanwhile, the Parliamentary Ombudsman said that many "have to borrow money from family and friends to support their children, using up their life's savings or running up credit card debts in order to pay for childcare costs, buy food and get to work"[149].

Of the six million families receiving tax credits in 2003-4, 1.9m were overpaid and a further 700,000 were underpaid. This means that nearly half of all tax credit recipients were either under or overpaid, triggering huge disruptions in people's lives and much chaos.

The problem with the tax and benefit system is that even when it works as intended, its effects are damaging. Perhaps one of the most chilling publications from the ONS is its annual Tax Benefit Model Tables, designed to illustrate the weekly financial circumstances of a selection of hypothetical local authority and private tenants.[150] The tables are produced from a spreadsheet-based model which calculates

148 *Money with your name on it?*, June 2005,
   http://www.citizensadvice.org.uk/index/campaigns/social_policy/evidence_reports/er_benefitsandtaxcredits.htm
149 *Tax Credits: Putting Things Right*, June 2005, http://www.ombudsman.org.uk/pdfs/tax_credits.pdf
150 Tax Benefit Model Tables, ONS and DWP, April 2005.

the interaction between income tax, National Insurance, tax credits and certain benefits. They demonstrate that taxes, NICs and benefits have a devastating effect on incentives and often almost completely sever the link between work and reward, especially for the worse-off and at lower income ranges. Marginal deduction rates of over 100% are not unheard of and rates of 70% or even 85% are common. Figure 14 illustrates the interaction of tax, tax credits and benefits faced by a traditional married family with two young children living in the private sector.

FIGURE 14: WHY IT DOES NOT PAY TO WORK

Married Deduction Rates

Married Couple with 2 children under 11, Private Tenant

Gross earnings £ per week		Marginal Deduction Rates
50.99	Income reduces HB/CTB	85.0%
94.00	NI becomes payable	87.9%
94.13	Tax payable at 10%	88.1%
100.13	WTC reduced by pay	93.7%
134.33	Tax payable at 22%	95.5%
266.79	WTC diaappears/CTC reduced by pay	95.5%
275.06	CTB disappears	89.5%
616.15	HB disappears	33.0%
630.00	NI Upper Earnings Limit (UEL)	23.0%
717.21	Tax payable at 40%	41.0%
958.91	CTC family element reduced by pay	47.7%
1,108.91	CTC disappears	41.0%

Married Couple with 2 children under 11, Private Tenant

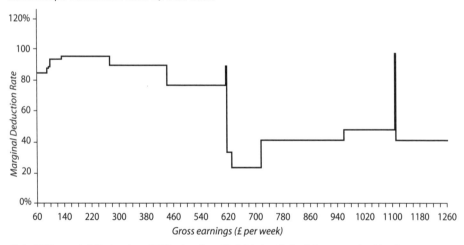

Note: MDRs may briefly rise above 100% where benefits fall below their minimum payment level

HB: Housing Benefit   CTB: Council Tax Benefit   NI: National Insurance contributions
WTC: Working Tax Credit   CTC: Child Tax Credit

Source: Office for National Statistics and Department for Work and Pensions [151]

---

151 Tax Benefit Model Tables.

According to estimates from the Lib Dems, 40% of pensioners pay marginal rate of tax and benefit withdrawal of over 50%; and 1.9m working households compared to 760,000 in 1998 (the position is even worse if housing benefit is included).[152]

Under a flat tax, tax credits would all be abolished. The critical question of how to tackle Britain's growing dependency on the government is one that is too great to be dealt with in this book. But given that the poorest would be taken out of the tax system, fewer benefits would be needed if the aim were to ensure that the income of the lower-paid remained the same or improved. However, for the purpose of the calculations in book, I assume that that the credits are wholly replaced by welfare benefits.

In the past, some flat tax proposals, such as that from Milton Friedman, were accompanied by a proposal for symmetrical negative income tax.[153] All income over a certain threshold would be taxed at a flat rate; income under a certain limit would be topped up. How this differs from the current failed tax credit system would be something worth exploring, though this remains outside the scope of this book.

Charitable donations, savings and pensions

Under a flat tax, tax deductions and other features of the tax code that favour charitable donations would be swept away. While this may hit charities in the short term, the overall dynamic effects of the flat tax will help charities in the longer-term. This is because buoyant economic growth will lead to a larger economy, allowing more money to be spared for charitable donations; the historical evidence suggests that donations to charities are most closely related to economic growth.[154] A flat tax would also promote entrepreneurial attitudes and wealth creation: after a few years of a flat tax, there would be many more very wealthy people in the UK. As the experience of the US has shown, multi-millionaires and billionaires like to make large donations to charity and to set up foundations to ensure they are remembered after their death. A flat tax would thus contribute to the promotion of a philanthropic culture in Britain.

A flat tax would also see the abolition of specialised savings vehicles such as individual savings accounts (ISAs) in the UK, as well as the existing huge tax incentives for pension provision. But this would not matter. Under Hall-Rabushka, payments on dividends would become tax free, to avoid the double taxation of corporate profits; and capital gains tax on equities would also be abolished. Individuals would also enjoy zero tax on interest payments; the tax would be paid at corporate level as the deductibility of interest from taxable profits would cease. On balance, it would be much easier to save and invest under a flat tax than under the current system, which combines high taxes on capital with a myriad of complex vehicles to avoid paying tax. There is no room here to address retirement policy; suffice to say that it matters not one jot whether saving takes

152 Liberal Democrat Federal Policy Committee (2005), op.cit
153 Friedman, op. cit.
154 Forbes, op. cit.

place through a vehicle called "pensions" or whether it takes place in other ways. A flat tax would promote the latter option.

Unlike in the US and many other countries, where mortgage interest payments are deductible from income for tax purposes, this practice has now been discontinued in the UK. This means one fewer hurdle to a comprehensive flat tax.

The classical liberal case for a flat tax

According to many critics of the flat tax, the fact that every individual and every company would pay the same share of their income or profits (or so they claim) would be unfair, unjust, or inequitable. They also argue that it is self-evident that those who earn more should pay more tax than those who are worse off.

The problem with the first argument is that under a flat tax with a large untaxed personal allowance, a large degree of progressivity remains (see the penultimate chapter of this book). The second argument is really an attack against a poll tax, not against a flat tax. Under a poll tax, everybody pays exactly the same amount of money, irrespective of circumstances, wealth, consumption or earnings. But under a pure proportional income tax with no personal allowance, someone who earns £100 pounds pays 10 times more tax than someone who earns £10; with a personal allowance the poor pay nothing and everybody else pays the flat tax rate.

Regardless of any of this, supporters of the flat tax should fight back and argue that it is fair, not unfair to impose the same tax rate on everybody, as long as a personal allowance is maintained. Everybody should be equal under the law; it is graduated income tax rates that are unfair.

Supporters of a flat tax should also go a step further. A fixation on the morality or otherwise of the flat tax itself (i.e. of the process by which taxes are raised) is a mistake; it would be much better to focus on how a flat tax boosts growth and therefore increases the size of the economy and creates more jobs and wealth for everyone, including the poor (i.e. its outcome). Slashing the top rate of tax would trigger a massive economic boom. Many top entrepreneurs and business leaders currently paying 41% tax including the top rate of National Insurance contributions would see their income more than double, compensating for the reduction in tax revenues. The gains would, as always, trickle down to everybody, as faster economic growth and increased investment would trigger an acceleration in productivity growth, job creation, and hence wages and living standards.

Opponents of the flat tax often claim that there is a diminishing marginal utility of income – as an individual gets wealthier, the marginal utility from earning an additional pound becomes less. The argument is that taking £10 from a highly paid individual is less painful than taking £10 from a poor person; therefore, the argument goes, high marginal rates of tax are good from the perspective of society as a whole because they provide plenty of additional utils to the poor while only sacrificing a limited number of the rich people's utils.

In the words of an economist at ING in London: "Economists pointed out that marginal increases in wealth were less important to the richest than to the poorest. If you have $1,000, an extra dollar is worth less than if you have just $100. Therefore, the greatest happiness for the greatest number would be better secured by taxing the rich more highly than the poor. Progressive income taxes were, therefore, more and more popular to politicians as the right to vote came into existence and was extended beyond the rich elite".[155]

There are several counter-arguments to this. The first is that it is simply not possible to assume that the rich would automatically not suffer (or suffer less than the poor) from a drop in their income, at least without knowing people's circumstances: someone on £100,000 who suffers a sudden 10% drop in his income due to higher taxes would most likely be plunged into crisis, such as being forced to default on his mortgage, in the same way as if this were to happen to someone making only £20,000 a year. House prices and living standards may differ; but an arbitrary and blanket assumption that the better-off wouldn't suffer from higher taxes is wrong because it doesn't take individual circumstances into account.

A related argument is more philosophical: some philosophers have argued that it is intellectually illegitimate to conduct so-called interpersonal comparisons of utility if utility is purely subjective.

Perhaps the most powerful counter-argument of all is to assume that the critics are right about the diminishing marginal utility of income – but to push the argument to its logical conclusion. If a wealthy person doesn't value an additional £10 very highly but values leisure a lot at his high level of income – as economists who have tried to measure the elasticity of labour have discovered to be the case, as we saw above – putting up the marginal tax rate on the wealthy will have a very important effect on their work effort. As one moves up the income scale, the relative power of the substitution effect compared to the income effects shifts in favour of the former – thus strengthening the case for the flat tax and highlighting the destructiveness of graduated tax systems, given that high-income individuals are the most likely to be job-creators and to employ other people.

The left-wing case for a flat tax

The claim that it would be unfair or morally wrong to scrap the current system of so-called progressive taxation (whereby tax rates go up with income) and move towards a proportional tax system (whereby someone who earns 10 times more pays 10 times more tax) is equally misguided.

---

155 'Flat tax rate', *Directional Economics*, June 2004, ING, London.

For a start, as the Treasury itself has acknowledged, a flat tax combined with a personal allowance is still progressive: there are in effect two tax rates, including one at 0%. The zero-rated allowance means that most flat taxes are progressive rather than proportional, though they gradually become more proportional at higher income ranges as the effective rate of tax approaches the marginal rate of tax.

There are plenty of other reasons why a flat tax would in fact be much fairer than the current system: it would allow many poor people to stop paying income tax (and under my favourite scheme, also national insurance contributions) altogether thanks to a bigger personal allowance and it would prevent those with better access to lawyers from paying less than the rest. At present, the bottom 20% of the population pays 5.2% of its income in income tax and NICs; these people would be better off under most flat tax plans. It is also arguably unfair that people who have the most money in the first place are able to enjoy greater tax breaks and tax reliefs than the poor, especially when it comes to pension contributions.

One peculiar – and for egalitarians, a desirable – side effect of flat taxes is that the better-off usually end up paying a larger share of total tax revenues than under a so-called progressive tax system. While this is very counter-intuitive, especially to those brought up on up on left-wing nostrums, it nevertheless makes sense both in terms of logic and economic theory, and it has been confirmed by every major tax cut in the UK and US. The evidence from countries that have implemented these schemes or that have radically cut tax rates is that taxpayers in the highest brackets shifted money from consumption or tax-sheltered investments into more productive, taxable investments. Many higher earners work harder or take additional risks, rewarded by higher after-tax returns.

It is not widely understood that the best way to get the better-off to pay more is to tax them less, as proved by every tax cutting government in history. Starting in 1979, when the top rate of tax was slashed from 98% including investment income to 75% (or 60% with no investment income), high–earning individuals soon started paying a higher percentage of the total tax take, encouraged by further regular reductions in the top rate. In 1984, the investment surcharge was abolished, cutting the top rate to 60%; then in 1988 the higher rate of income tax was cut again to 40%. During that time, the top 10% of earners went from paying a 35% share of total revenues collected in 1979 to 42% by 1990.[156] This has continued to increase, reaching an expected 52% in 2005-06, according to figures from HMRC.[157] Another way to look at this is to say that in 1978-79, 21% of taxpayers paid half of total receipts, compared with under 10% of the top-earners today.[158]

America's tax cutting episodes saw a similar phenomenon. Taxes paid by those making $50,000 or more climbed from 44.2% of the total burden in 1921 to 78.4% in 1928. During the tax cuts of the 1960s, collections from those making over $50,000 per

156 Grecu, Andrei (2004), *Flat Tax – The British Case*, Adam Smith Institute, London, www.adamsmith.org/pdf/flattax.pdf
157 HMRC, Shares of total income tax liability, 2005-06, Table 2.4, http://www.hmrc.gov.uk/stats/income_tax/table2-4.pdf
158 Analysis from Lombard Street Research

year climbed by 57% between 1963 and 1966, while tax collections from those earning below $50,000 rose 11% — even though, once again, the top rate of tax was slashed. The rich saw their portion of the income tax burden climb from 11.6% to 15.1%. And under Ronald Reagan, the share of income taxes paid by the top 10% jumped from 48% in 1981 to 57.2% in 1988. The top 1% saw their share of the income tax bill explode from 17.6% in 1981 to 27.5% in 1988.

In Canada, Alberta adopted a 10% provincial flat tax on personal income in 2001. The new scheme includes a personal allowance for provincial income on the first $15,000 in earnings. The experience of the US means that nobody should be surprised to hear that the top 15% of Alberta earners now pay more than two-thirds of the province's income taxes — up from 63% the year before the single-rate tax was introduced. And the Alberta Treasury has suffered no revenue shock as a result of the new rates.[159]

The better-off would also end up paying a larger share of the total tax burden if a flat tax were introduced in Britain today because it would encourage a new generation of risk-takers and entrepreneurs to become rich. Getting rid of the top 40% rate would probably lead to a small reduction in the share of taxes paid by the top decile during the first year or so following the reform – but the proportion would soon shoot up again and overtake current levels. It is better for governments to take a smaller share of bigger pie than a big share of a small pie: everybody is better off in a bigger economy.

---

159 http://www.freedomandprosperity.org/blog/2005-09/2005-09.shtml#141

Chapter VI: Other countries

Traditionally, only small tax havens and countries such as the Channel Islands and Hong Kong have operated systems with strong similarities to the flat tax. Jersey and Guernsey switched from the British income tax code to a flat tax of 20%. In 1947, Hong Kong introduced a dual income tax system, allowing taxpayers to choose either to be taxed progressively on income adjusted for deductions and allowances; or to pay a flat tax on their gross income – as befits a country that until recent increases in government intervention and spending was the most perfect example of a capitalist nation. Its current flat tax rate is 16%.

The first country to make the jump in recent history was the tiny Baltic state of Estonia, which adopted a 26% flat rate of income tax in 1994. At the time, the country was led by Mart Laar - who had become prime minister two years earlier at the remarkable age of 32 - and his government of twenty-something radicals. In 2000, Estonia also reformed its company tax regime along flat-tax lines.

These days, Laar, who sports a splendid beard, travels the world making the case for the flat tax: while economists such as Rabushka are the tax's intellectual gurus, Laar is its leading political advocate. When I interviewed him last year, he forecast that within five years all eastern and central European countries will have adopted the flat tax - a possibility which looks less fanciful by the day.

Ever since the tiny Baltic state of Estonia decided to turn its back once and for all on Communism and adopted a flat tax on personal incomes in 1994, eight other ex-communist Central and Eastern European countries have followed suit and adopted flat tax structures. These reforms vary in their degree of comprehensiveness and as we shall see, none is fully flat.[160]

After Estonia, the next country to junk a previously convoluted income tax code and embrace a flat tax was Latvia, another tiny Baltic state, in 1995. At 25%, the rate was chosen to undercut Estonia's; the fact that Latvia felt forced to follow Estonia's lead confirms the power of tax competition and the need for countries to attract capital. Neighbouring Lithuania also moved towards a flat-tax system, with a 33% rate on wage and salary income, but it continues to impose a wide variety of rates depending on source of income.

After the Baltic states, the flat tax's momentum stalled for a while. But Estonia's economy became an international success story, attracting the attention of Andrei Illarionov, Russian president Vladimir Putin's economic adviser. Eventually, Russia stunned the world when it announced a flat tax on personal incomes in 2001 at a single marginal rate of 13% above 4,800 Russian Rubles. Despite a corrupt and illiberal economic environment, the flat tax has been a key reason - in addition to soaring

---

160 For detailed information on some of the economic reforms in the region, see Grabowski, Maciej and Marcin Tomalak, *Tax system reforms in the countries of Central Europe and the Commonwealth of Independent States*, http://www.warsawvoice.pl/krynica2004/Special%20Study.pdf

commodity prices - why the Russian economy has grown strongly over the past four years.

In a mere four years, total receipts more than doubled, despite the reduced tax rate, an increase which has far outstripped that of the economy as a whole. Unsurprisingly, some politicians and international bodies (and notably the IMF[161]) have claimed that this surge in revenues had little to do with the flat tax and all to do with a crackdown on tax evasion. They are right to question whether all the revenue increase came from the flat tax – it didn't, of course, but nobody is claiming that – but the truth is that there is plenty of reliable international evidence that lower taxes boost economic growth.

Despite the criticism from some quarters, the Russian reforms were highly influential because of the size of the country and its status as the region's former imperial superpower, and half a dozen other countries promptly followed suit when they realised that Russia's flat tax was a resounding success.

The first was Serbia in 2003, which introduced a 14% tax on income and corporate profits; it is set to cut this rate further. Next came Ukraine, which also chose a 13% flat rate; from this year dividends and bank interest are taxed at only 5%. In 2004, Slovakia implemented a 19% flat tax on income and company profits. Rabushka, who counts Slovakia's flat tax as one of his favourites, says: "It greatly simplified the previous system which included 90 exceptions, 19 sources of income that were not taxed, 66 items that were tax exempt and 27 items with their own specific tax rates, such as bank interest and honoraria. Once the corporate tax is paid, dividends received by individuals are tax free." Slovakia's is the most comprehensive flat tax structure to date with Personal Income Tax, Corporate Tax and VAT all taxed at the same rate.

In the past few months, Romania and Georgia joined the bandwagon to ensure they remained attractive to global investors. Georgia introduced a 12% flat rate of income tax, which came into effect on 1 January 2005, cutting the size and weight of the old tax code by 95%. While the reforms retained the 20% profit tax, they cut social insurance from 33% to 20% and VAT from 20% to 18%. And as a result of the intense competition from its newly competitive neighbours, Estonia has just cut its flat income tax by two percentage points to 24% and has promised that the tax will fall to 20% in two years' time. In December 2004, when Trajan Basecu was elected president of Romania in a surprise victory, his first decision was to adopt a radical flat tax of 16% for both personal income and corporate profits, throwing away an incomprehensible Western-style tax code with rates from 18% to 40% for individuals. Even more astonishingly, the reforms became effective on 1 January 2005, three days after Basecu unveiled his detailed plans, almost certainly setting a new record for speedy policy implementation!

Today, four European Union member states operate flat taxes, thus thumbing

---

161 Ivanova, Keen, and Klemm, op. cit.

their noses at the harmonising tendency in Brussels: these are – in order of adoption – Estonia, Lithuania, Latvia and Slovakia. Following Slovakia's radical move, the debate over the potential benefits of a flat tax has become intense in neighbouring countries, especially the Czech Republic, Poland and Hungary. Not only is their competitiveness now most obviously at risk but they are interested in Slovakia as a case study of a post-communist, transition economy successfully overhauling its economy.

In the Czech Republic, the opposition wants an integrated 15% flat tax on companies and individuals. In Slovenia, work on a flat tax is at an advanced stage, with the final proposal likely to include flat but different rates for income tax, corporation tax and value added tax. There is also some interest in Hungary and Bulgaria.

It seems that West European governments remain attached for the time being at least to the destructive principle of graduated taxation, wrongly seen as an efficient tool for wealth redistribution. That said, tax rates are becoming flatter, top rates are being cut and the number and complexity of tax bands is continuing to be reduced. The debate on the flat tax continues in the old Member States, and particularly in those with neighbouring countries that have already moved in that direction themselves.

As the Treasury itself has been forced to acknowledge: "The concept of a flat rate of income tax has been growing in popularity over the last few years as more and more Eastern European countries have adopted it, and it has been floated in more developed countries like Germany and the US have considered the idea. There has been a growing interest in the UK too".

Australia, Austria, Denmark, Finland, Greece, Italy and Spain have also seen debates or proposals made on moving towards a flat tax. In other Western European states, although there is no current move towards adopting a pure flat tax structure, the trend for cutting top rates and reducing the number and complexity of tax bands is continuing strongly. Most remarkably of all, Rabushka recently travelled to China on the invitation of the finance ministry to outline his ideas. His book has been translated into Chinese and published with a preface by Lou Jiwei, the vice minister of finance. Top Chinese academics have also endorsed the idea.

In the US, many leading conservatives are enamoured with the idea and President Bush wants to push through radical tax reform in his second term. There are currently several bills before the House of Representatives, including one which proposes a flat 17% tax with a generous personal allowance. A Flat Tax bill has been under consideration by the House Ways and Means Committee since 1997. Unfortunately, partly because Congress is unlikely to abolish tax relief on mortgage payments for the foreseeable future, the best that can realistically be hoped for is a further flattening of the income tax code.

In its recent analysis of the flat tax, released under Britain's new freedom of information legislation, the Treasury was at pains to point out that close scrutiny often reveals that the actual tax system in Eastern Europe is rather more complex than low headline flat tax rates would suggest. While they were right and no country in the world has introduced a fully comprehensive flat tax, this does not mean that such a system is not desirable or feasible; nor that it couldn't work.

The problem is that there are many additional taxes to be paid on top of income tax. Hong Kong currently has a flat tax of 16% but it generates a lot of its tax revenue through its property tax on the 'net assessable value' of a property (or how much the property could be rented for). In the Slovak Republic and Romania, high social security payments complement the official income tax. And Global Insight, the top economic consultancy, said: "Like those of other countries in the region, Romania's payroll taxes remain a disincentive to investment, despite the attractiveness of the flat tax."[162] As John Chown puts it: "flat tax regimes are usually distorted by the impact of Social Security contributions (the equivalent of National Insurance in the UK) which have grown up as a thinly disguised form of secondary income tax".[163] The table below summarises the evidence (the figures for social security contributions are approximate and not necessarily top marginal rates).

FIGURE 15: FLAT TAXES IN EASTERN EUROPE

Date of launch	Country	Personal income tax	Corporate income tax	Social contributions
1994	Estonia	24% (originally 26%, 20% by 2007)	0 retained 26 distributed	33.5%+1%
1994	Lithuania	33% wages/salaries, other income 15%	15%	31%+3%
1995	Latvia	25%	19% (to fall to 15%)	24.09%+9%
2000	Russia	13%	24%	28.2% minimum
2003	Serbia and Montenegro	14%	10%	17.9%+17.9%
2004	Slovakia	19%	19%	34.4%+13.4%
2004	Ukraine	13% (to rise to 15%)	25%	36.8%+3.5%
2005	Georgia	12%	20%	20%
2005	Romania	16%	16%	33.5%+17%

Note: the data are from a variety of sources and tax and social security contribution figures are simplified; social security rates are not applicable to all income levels and so cannot simply be added to income tax; social security contributions are given for employers and employees.

Chown calculates the effective tax rates for several of the main Eastern European countries. He finds that their effective tax rates (income tax plus employers and employee social security contributions) is much higher than is commonly understood. The effective tax

162 Global Insight, op. cit
163 Chown, op. cit.

rate is 44.36% in Estonia, 39.52% in Latvia, 51.15% in Lithuania, 50.56% in Slovakia. This sounds very high but the situation in the UK is even worse: adding in employee and employer NICs generates a maximum tax rate of 53.8% (but a top marginal rate of 41%). In Russia, the effective tax rate is 30.95% on the first 280,000 rubles, 20.91% on the next 320,000 rubles and then 14.71% on the balance over 600,000, he argues. This suggests that the full economic benefits of the flat tax will have been emasculated.

There is another problem with the Eastern European reforms. According to the UK Treasury, in the new EU member states personal income tax accounts for 14.4% of total tax revenue, compared with a figure of 24.1% for the EU-15, which has meant reductions in the tax rate in Eastern European countries have not had significant effects on the overall tax take.

The recent experience of Poland and Slovakia in introducing radical tax reforms suggests that impacts on countries' budgets are limited, according to the Economist Intelligence Unit.[164] It argues that the Polish and Slovak examples show that the switch to low or flat rates is unlikely to undermine revenue dramatically. This is not simply down to Laffer curve dynamics. It also reflects the fact that the share of income tax and corporation tax in those countries' overall tax revenues is quite low.

Despite the limitations of the Eastern European reforms, it is clear that the time is ripe for flat taxes. Even when payroll taxes and social security contributions are added, tax rates are increasingly lower than in the UK. Following a "research trip" to Estonia in June 2005, George Osborne, the UK Shadow Chancellor said: "It would be difficult to introduce a flat tax regime in Britain but we all need to realise the competitive pressures we face in the 21st century." And when President Bush visited Slovakia earlier this year, he was full of praise for their tax reforms. With a bit of luck, any Western country that decides to follow suit will go even further. In the remainder of this chapter, each flat tax country is analysed in turn.

Estonia

Estonia introduced its version of the flat tax in 1994. For the first ten years, from 1994 to 2004, the rate for personal income was 26%. In December 2003, the Estonian government decided to cut the rate to 24% from 1 January 2005, to 22% from 1 January 2006 and 20% from 1 January 2007 in a bid to stay ahead of the rest of the region. Since 1 January 2005, the basic annual exemption for an individual who resides in Estonia is EEK 20,400, a sum which will rise to EEK 24,000 from 1 January 2006.[165] Income tax revenues are split 11.4% to local authorities with the rest going to the central government.

According to one of the authors of the recently-released UK Treasury documents

164 *Economist Intelligence Unit*, op. cit.
165 See tax country note on Estonia from Ernst and Young and Taxes at a Glance, Eastern European edition, PricewaterhouseCoopers.

on the flat tax: "My contact stated that there were no transitional problems in moving to the flat rate, instead it helped to solve existing problems such as the high inflation rate which led to changing levels of income for each tax bracket".[166]

As with every other country that has adopted a variant of the flat tax, there is unfortunately more to Estonia's tax code than that. In addition to income tax, companies and individuals must pay social security contributions. In the Estonian case, however, these are overwhelmingly concentrated on companies. A social tax at a very high level of 33% is levied on the salaries of employees, payable by employers, with no ceiling. An additional 0.5% unemployment insurance tax is paid by employers, as well as 1% by employees. So the combined rate of tax for individuals is 25%, rather than the 24% headline rate, though this remains very low by British standards.

Where the Estonian flat tax breaks completely down is for the self-employed. They have to pay the 33% social tax on net income themselves – the argument being that they are their own employers, and that not doing so would incentivise everybody to become self-employed. Although this may be seen as fair and is true in narrowly economic terms, it makes self-employment very difficult in practice. Self-employed people also pay income tax at 24% based on their annual income from trading. This is the worst of both worlds.

Of the 33% social security contributions, health represents 13% and pension funding 20%. A direct link remains between social tax paid by the employer and benefit entitlement of the employee to state pension, sickness benefits and other social guarantees (however, social tax paid on fringe benefits does not increase social and health insurance benefits).

The Estonian government's long-term aim is to move towards lower tax on labour and to increase consumption-related and other indirect taxes. The idea is that excise duties and environmental taxes will probably be hiked, whereas income tax will continue to fall. They also want to maintain the current simple tax system and broad tax base while improving tax administration.

There are no inheritance or gift taxes in Estonia, though gifts from non-resident entities are taxed at 24%. Capital gains tax from the sale of business property or securities are also taxed at 24%.

One of the most interesting aspects of the Estonian tax system is that tax is not charged on undistributed corporate profits, but only on distributions (both actual and deemed), including profits handed back to shareholders in the form of dividends and other profit distributions, fringe benefits, gifts, donations, representation expenses and expenses that taxman deems are unrelated to its business activity. In 2005, such distributions are subject to a 24/76 tax. This is set to be gradually reduced by 2009, by which time distributed corporate income will be taxed at a flat 20/80 rate.

What this system means is that corporate tax is not paid immediately,

---

166 HM Treasury, op. cit.

investment spending is tax-free and there is no double taxation of dividends. Although the mechanics are different from those envisaged in Hall-Rabushka, the end result is very similar. Importantly, income and expenses are accounted for in the year they occur – so as accountants have pointed out, this makes it virtually a cash flow tax.

There is also a zero tax rate on dividends to non-resident corporate shareholders that own at least one-fifth of the shares or votes of a resident company (if they own less than 20%, then they have to pay a 24% withholding tax).

Value added tax is charged at a standard rate of 18%, though there are also reduced rates of 5% and 0%.

The Estonian flat tax system does suffer from some exemptions and special cases. There is a 10% tax rate for certain benefits from voluntary pension schemes; and a 15% final withholding tax on certain payments to non-residents. There are also some other indirect taxes and a number of local taxes. Additional exemptions apply to state pensioners and people with 3 or more children.

Foreign direct investment has more than quadrupled in Estonia since introducing a flat tax, from an inflow of $202m in 1995 to $926m in 2004, according to the United Nations Conference on Trade and Development's Foreign Direct Investment Database.

There is much that Britain and other rich countries can learn from Estonia, especially the fact that only distributed profits are taxed and the fact that the system is close to being a cash flow tax. The main drawback is the high levels of social security contributions. Estonia's 1999 Income Tax Act was only 72 pages long.

Latvia

Following the introduction of Latvia's version of the flat tax, companies pay a 15% flat tax on profits.[167] Individuals are charged a flat tax of 25% on their personal income. However, there are also hefty social security contributions, the bulk of which are picked up by employers who are landed with a 24.09% tax. Employees have to pay an additional 9%.

VAT is charged at 18%, with a lower 5% rate applicable to certain goods and services such as medical supplies and newspapers.

On top of that, Latvians are also subject to a property tax of 1.5% on land, buildings and structures (excluding private homes, which are exempt).

Dividends received by residents from Latvian companies are not taxed; interest paid by Latvians banks to residents and non-residents alike is not taxed. Latvia does generally not charge capital gains tax on the sale of property, though real estate owned for less than a year is taxable. There are also no inheritance, estate or gift taxes, though state authorities may impose a duty on the value of an inheritance at rates of between 0.5% and 3%.

---

167 See Ernst & Young, country note on Latvia; PricewaterhouseCoopers, op. cit.

Latvia's tax policies on dividends and interest payments are especially noteworthy and economically beneficial.

Lithuania

Lithuania imposes a 15% tax on taxable profits for most companies, but it also has a 13% reduced rate on the taxable profits of small companies with fewer than 10 workers or a very small turnover.

Income tax is charged at 33% for employment income and a reduced rate of 15% for other income.[168] Employers have to pay an additional 31% in social security contributions and employees 3%. Dividends from local and foreign companies alike are taxed at 15%.

The main rate of VAT is 18%, though there are also reduced rates of 9%, 5% and 0%. Property taxes are important to the Lithuanian exchequer. A real estate tax of 1% is levied on the value of immovable property owned by entities. Entities that own land are subject to land tax at a rate of 1.5% of the value of the land. Finally, state-owned land that is leased is subject to a land lease tax at a rate of 1.5%-4%.

As a result of this hodge-podge of rates, Alvin Rabushka doesn't consider Lithuania to have a proper flat tax.[169]

But Lithuania may move to a more radical flat tax of 24% on income by 2008, according to Prime Minister Algirdas Brazauskas. Brazauskas said that this would be to move Lithuania into line with other countries in central and eastern Europe.[170]

Russia

Undoubtedly the most significant country to have adopted a flat-tax style regime is Russia. Although its overall tax system remains further from the Hall-Rabushka ideal than that of some of the other Eastern European nations, it is much more rational and efficient than it used to be.

The general income tax rate is 13% but there are plenty of exceptions. The main flat rate of corporate income tax is 24% of taxable profit.[171]

Dividends paid to Russian residents are eligible for a tax of 9%; non-residents must hand over 30%. Interest on money in Russian accounts that is greater than the central bank's refinancing rate on ruble deposits, as well as interest on money in foreign currency deposits, is taxed at a hefty 35%. A 35% tax rate has also been slapped on certain insurance pay-outs and deemed income from loans with very low interest rates

---

168 See Ernst & Young, country note on Lithuania; PricewaterhouseCoopers, op. cit.
169 'A competitive flat tax may spread to Lithuania', Alvin Rabushka, *RussianEconomy.org*, 24 March 2005:
    http://www.russianeconomy.org/comments/032405.html
170 'Lithuania aims for 24 pct flat tax by 2008', *The Washington Times*, 24 March 2005:
    http://washingtontimes.com/upi-breaking/20050324-102603-7269r.htm
171 See Ernst & Young, country note on Russia; PricewaterhouseCoopers, op. cit.

and on certain material benefits.

For all other income, Russian residents pay a 13% flat rate of tax while non-residents pay a flat 30% rate.

There is also a unified social tax of 26% for salaries of between 0 and 280,000 rubles a year, paid by the employer. In addition, there is a 2% extra tax starting at 600,000 rubles a year. Employers are also hit with an accident insurance contribution of between 0.2% and 8.5%; the exact rate depends on the kind of job. Value added tax is charged at 18% on most goods and services, with reduced rates of 10% and zero. There are also regional and local property taxes slapped on the value of property, land or fixed assets, as well as a car tax and other levies.

According to the UK Treasury, when Russia introduced its 13% flat income tax, revenue as a percentage of GDP increased by a fifth. This increase would not cover the loss of revenue in the UK, the Treasury claims.

Taxpayers also enjoy a number of deductions. The first is that they don't pay tax on their first R400 a month – more if they are veterans, suffer from certain disabilities or belong to other special groups. However, this R400 deduction only applies to those making less than 20,000 rubles per month. There are also a number of social tax deductions for charitable contributions and educational and medical expenses, as well as tax reductions on some property expenses.

As a rule, capital gains are taxed like other income and there is no separate capital gains tax. But gains on the sale of property owned for more than three years is not subjected to tax.

The Duma voted on 15 June 2005 to abolish inheritance tax to take effect on 1 January 2006. At present, estates are taxed at between 5% and 40%. Russia also abolished gift tax to close relatives, including spouses, parents, children, grandparents, grandchildren, siblings, and step-siblings, currently taxed at between 3% and 15%. The reform also slashed gifts to non-family members from a tax rate of 10%-40%, bringing it in line with the flat rate of 13%.[172]

Alvin Rabushka has studied the effects of the Russian flat tax experiment in great depth and has explained how income tax receipts have exploded following its introduction, growing faster than overall revenues and other taxes. In 2004, personal income tax revenues reached 574.1bn rubles, a huge 26.1% surge compared with 2003. After controlling for consumer price inflation of 11.7%, real revenues surged 14.4%, significantly faster than real economic growth. Real receipts from personal income tax surged by 25.2% in 2001, 24.6% in 2002 and 15.2% in 2003. For the four years, Rabushka calculates that the compound real ruble revenue is up a remarkable 105.6%.

172 'Russia Abolishes Inheritance Tax', Alvin Rabushka, RussianEconomy.org, 20 June 2005:
http://www.russianeconomy.org/comments/062005.html

Rabushka said:

"The 26.1% nominal growth in personal income tax receipts outpaced the overall 24.7% rise in total taxes and fees in 2004. As a share of total taxes and revenue, it rivals payments for use of natural resources, is more than double excises, and now stands at 76.6% of value added tax. The most dramatic change in 2004 is the 64.5% rise in nominal rubles, or 52.8% in real rubles, in corporate taxes".[173]

The main criticism of the Russian reforms is to be found in the paper recently published by the IMF and cited earlier.[174] The paper argues that the flat tax wasn't responsible for the surge of revenues identified by economists such as Rabushka.

The most interesting findings of the IMF paper are not its conclusions, which are questionable, but the fact that they find tax rates actually didn't fall very much in Russia despite the introduction of the flat tax – largely because exemptions were abolished. The paper finds that the average effective rate of personal income tax actually went up from 11.2% to 11.8%; the average effective tax rate inclusive of employer paid taxes decreased by only 2.5 percentage points. What this suggests is that the effects of the flat tax on work effort are likely to have been limited – but only because the reforms didn't go far enough.

The authors base their conclusions on an annual survey which provides information on the incomes and other attributes of around 3,500 adults. The authors admit that the information provided is not ideal but argue that it matches closely macroeconomic data. However, they also admit that the distribution of incomes in their sample is such that very few people saw their marginal tax rates fall noticeably under the flat tax. While the authors try to compensate for this, this remains problematic. Only eleven taxpayers in the sample paid tax at the 30% before the reform, for example.

The authors summarise their findings thus: "Whether or not one takes account of tax evasion and misreporting of true incomes in the data, the evidence is that the 2001 reform led to much lower tax revenues from affected individuals—suggesting that the revenue boom which followed was not caused by it. When investigating further the effect on incomes, we find that while the reform reduced gross wage rates, had no measurable effect on labour supply, it strongly boosted compliance".

Regardless of whether or not the authors are right about labour supply, better compliance is a key prediction of flat tax supporters – but although they find an increase of around 16 percentage points in the proportion of income declared by those affected by the reform, the authors are unable to judge whether it was caused by the reform or a crackdown on tax evasion by the authorities.

173 'The Flat Tax at Work in Russia: Year Four, 2004', Alvin Rabushka, *RussianEconomy.org*, 26 January 2005:
    http://www.russianeconomy.org/comments/012605.html
174 Ivanova, Keen, and Klemm, op. cit.

The authors' data set, their finding that tax rates barely fell and the existence of so much other evidence which shows that higher earners are in fact incentivised by lower tax rates means that the paper ultimately fails to convince.

Serbia and Montenegro

Serbia operates a flatish tax system, albeit one which charges different rates for different types of income. It is therefore much more complicated than under the pure system envisaged by Hall and Rabushka. There is a 14% flat rate of income tax on salaries; 10% on the net earnings of the self-employed; 16% on grants and loans from employers to help pay school fees above a certain monthly level; and 20% for other income, including dividends, capital gains, royalties, directors fees and income from property leasing.[175] There is no tax on interest on government bonds and interest on demand deposits. Serb residents for tax purposes can benefit from a 50% reduction in their tax on dividends; entrepreneurs also pay half the capital gains tax rate. Company profits are taxed at flat and low rate of 10%. There are three rates of VAT: 0%, 8% and 18%.

The personal allowance is set at 40% of the average wage. In addition, taxpayers enjoy an extra deduction worth 15% of the average annual salary per dependent. The total deductions from the personal allowance and the dependents allowance is limited to 50% of the annual average salary.

There are also property taxes, inheritance tax and gift tax. Property tax ranges from 0.4% to 3%of the value of the assets owned or rented, which can be very steep. Inheritance tax is progressive and ranges between 3% and 5%, which is tiny by UK standards. The transfer tax ranges from 0.3% to 5%.

But while all of these tax rates are quite low, they are unfortunately accompanied by oppressively high social security contributions. Employees and employers both pay 11% to the pension and disability fund, 6.15% for health care, and 0.75% for unemployment insurance, totalling 17.9%. Social security contributions are even higher on some forms of income.

Slovakia

Slovakia is the most developed economy with a flat tax, and therefore provides the best comparison for the UK. President Bush praised Slovakia's flat tax during a recent trip there. "I really congratulate ... your government for making wise decisions," he said. Company tax and personal income tax are both charged at 19%, as is value added tax (though a 0% rate for VAT also exists on certain items).[176] Another important reform is

---

175 See Ernst & Young, country note on Serbia and Montenegro; PricewaterhouseCoopers, op. cit.
176 See Ernst & Young, country note on Slovakia; PricewaterhouseCoopers, op. cit.

that dividends are no longer taxable; and therefore corporate profits are no longer taxed twice. This is a major move towards a Hall-Rabushka system.

As ever, the main flaw in the Slovak plan is that social security charges – a form of income tax in all but name – remain very high: employers must pay 34.4% of remuneration capped at SKK 43,095. Employees have to pay 13.4% of remuneration, also capped at SKK 43,095. But at least these NICs are a flat tax; and because of the cap, they are in effect a regressive tax.

There is also a property tax imposed by local government, with no real limits and a rate that depends on how a property is used and where it is located. The tax per square metre on an office building in the capital is typically SKK 340 or EUR 8.5. The interest withholding tax has also been set at 19%, and is reduced by double tax treaties. There is a 0% tax on interest paid to related EU tax residents from 1 January 2005.

Slovakia's economy is set to grow by 4.9% this year and 5.2% next year, against 4.4% and 4.5% for Poland, and 4% and 4.2% for the Czech Republic. By late September, the Slovak Share Index was up 44% since the start of 2005 and up by more than 100% since the beginning of 2004.

The Slovak government believes that the launch of the flat-tax was key in securing a $1.3bn foreign investment in 2004 by Korea's car maker Hyundai, which is building a Kia factory in Zilina. Total foreign direct investment in Slovakia last year hit $13.6bn, six times more than in 1998. Matin Bruncko, chief economic adviser to Slovak Finance Minister Ivan Miklos, says "the flat [personal income] tax has made Slovakia more attractive for highly paid expatriate employees. That's important for companies looking at an offshore operation."[177]

In 2003, the Slovak government's trade development agency, SARIO, brought in 22 investment projects that created 7,500 new jobs. In 2004, this increased to 47 projects worth more than 12,700 jobs. Euro Valley Industrial Park, which lies on the highway to Prague, a half hour out of Bratislava, has become home to Italian tyre-maker Pirelli and multinational steel concern Arcelor, which are building facilities there. And last month, a joint venture between a German transmission-maker and Ford announced a $395 million investment in eastern Slovakia. The flat tax is "a very important factor," for these new companies, says Ivan Kocis, the park's co-chairman.[178] Ivan Miklos, Finance Minister and Deputy Prime Minister of Slovakia, says:

"The new Slovak tax system has been particularly popular with German companies. It has made Slovakia an even more attractive destination for their investment. Yet it has also contributed indirectly to the improved competitiveness of the German economy. For example, the concern that jobs

177 'Europe Circles The Flat Tax', *BusinessWeek*, 26 September 2005:
   http://www.businessweek.com/magazine/content/05_39/b3952079.htm
178 'Flat-tax movement stirs Europe', Andreas Tzorzis, *The Christian Science Monitor*, 8 March 2005:
   http://www.csmonitor.com/2005/0308/p01s03-woeu.html

would move east became one of the main incentives for liberalisation of labour relations in the German corporate sector"[179]

According to a paper commissioned by free market think tank Reform, after introducing a flat tax in 2004, tax revenues fell by only 0.2% of GDP, from 25.5% in 2003 to 25.3% in 2004, though this is partly as a result of raising indirect taxes. The consequence has been significantly higher economic growth, rising from an average of 3.4% in the six years preceding reform, to 5.5% in 2004 and 4.8% in 2005, according to information by Jaroslav Belas, Professor at the Economic University of Bratislava.[180]

The best analysis to date of the Slovak situation can be found in a recent report from ING, the Dutch investment bank.[181] The report notes that Slovakia has had an excellent record at cutting the tax and spending to GDP ratio over the past few years, transforming the make-up of the Slovak economy. Between 1995 and 2003, tax revenues and social security contributions fell by 10% of GDP, a remarkable achievement at a time when equivalent numbers for the EU as a whole remained almost completely unchanged.

FIGURE 16: SLOVAKIA'S FLAT TAX

% of GDP, first year of the reforms

	2003	2004 without reform	2004 Budget	2004E	Difference (estimate-budget)
Tax revenues	18.1	18.0	17.4	17.6	0.2
Personal Income taxes*	3.6	3.6	2.4	2.7	0.3
Corporate Income taxes*	3.3	3.4	2.2	2.6	0.3
VAT	6.7	7.2	8.6	8.0	-0.6
Excises	3.1	2.8	3.3	3.4	0.1
Other taxes	1.4	1.0	0.9	1.0	0.1

Source: ING, analysis based on MinFin (Institute of Financial Policy) figures.

As ING notes in its research, the introduction of the flat tax was not intended to be neutral for the budget in the short term and tax revenues declined by 0.5% of GDP in 2004. This was accompanied by reduced expenditures.

But as ING points out: "Even though the authorities had already assumed in the budget an ad-hoc slight increase in motivation to declare income taxes at a lower rate, the reality was a pleasant surprise".[182] Tax revenues turned out 0.6% of GDP higher than

179 *Financial Times*, 23 March 2005.
180 Unpublished paper on the Slovak tax reforms for Reform, July 2005, cited in Reform Bulletin, op. cit.; IMF, 2002 and 2005.
181 Flat tax update, *Directional Economics*, March 2005, ING, London
182 ING, op. cit.

forecast by the government, thanks to higher receipts from both personal income and corporate taxes. Receipts from VAT were disappointing, but this was unrelated to the flat tax and caused instead by changes in collection caused by EU membership.

The March 2005 ING report states:

"Interestingly, the flat tax regime has seen a better-than-expected increase in tax collection. The government was surprised to see that the flat tax is a huge marketing tool for foreign corporate investors. Slovakia is now a prime example of a transparent and simple tax system with very low tax rates. Presently, the tax regime is an important factor supporting FDI inflow to the country next to low labour costs, low asset prices, EU membership, etc. More investments mean more capacity and higher potential growth rates in the future. Even the opposition is gradually changing its negative view on the flat tax."

Charles Robertson, ING's chief economist for Emerging Europe, Middle East and Africa, and an opponent of the flat tax idea for the UK, points out that "in 2004 Slovak personal income tax collection dropped by 25%. Corporate tax receipts fell more than 20% as this rate was cut and unified at 19% too. Even a hike in value added tax to 19% for previously exempt products failed to make up the difference".[183] This is not particularly surprising: advocates of a flat tax do not believe the whole dynamic effect of a flat tax will be seen immediately.

A related explanation can be found in the main argument used by the UK Treasury and left-wing activists to attack the Slovak model. Their core argument is to add income tax with employees' as well as employers' National Insurance contributions and to compare this overall tax wedge in Slovakia to that in the UK. But what these critics do not realise is that they help to explain why there were fewer immediate supply-side effects on tax receipts in Slovakia than there were in Romania: the problem is that marginal tax rates remain far too high for comfort in Slovakia, despite being hidden from sight.

The Treasury has alleged that the Slovak Republic has combined Social Security contributions between 48.1% and 49.9%, "which is over twice the UK's highest rate". The Treasury also said in its assessment of the flat tax: "In the Slovak Republic an individual on 100% of average earnings takes home 58% compared to the UK, where an individual takes home 69%. In Slovakia personal income tax contributes to only 2% GDP in the UK this is 10%".[184]

Richard Murphy and John Christensen, of the left-wing Tax Justice Network, said: "If it is assumed that the employer's contribution comes out of the total

183 'Flat tax: comparisons with Slovakia are more valid for the UK', Charles Robertson, *Financial Times*, 5 September 2005
184 HM Treasury, op. cit.

remuneration budget available to employees, then the combined rate of tax and social security contributions for an employee in Slovakia is exactly 50% as opposed to a practical maximum similar rate of 47.7% for those earning more than about £37,000 in the UK and 40.6% for most earning below that sum".[185] However, if we assume no contracting out of national insurance contributions in the UK, as we saw earlier, the combined rate in the UK is actually well over 50%, still lower than those cited for Sovakia by Murphy and Christensen.

Despite the undoubted limitations of the Slovak reforms, which have not yet gone far enough, the Slovak economy is nevertheless much better off and enjoys hugely improved incentives compared with the previous tax system.

Ukraine

Like in neighbouring Russia, Ukraine currently levies a 13% flat rate of tax on income for residents (but this is expected to go up to 15% in 2007); non-residents pay twice that[186]. The tax on corporate profits is currently 25%. Dividends are also charged at 13% but stock dividends are exempt. There is no tax on interest payments until 2010, when a 5% charge will be levied. Capital gains tax is also usually charged.

As ever, there are also huge social security taxes. Employers pay 36.8%, which includes 32.3% for pensions, 2.9% for social security and 1.6% for unemployment insurance – but the income on which this is charged is capped at UAH 4,100 per employee per month. There is also a charge to cover insurance for workplace-related accidents which varies from 0.2% to 13.8%, depending on the industry. Employees pay 3.5% in social security contributions. Value added tax is charged at up to 20%.

Georgia

On 22 December 2004, Georgia's parliament tore up the country's tax code and introduced a 12% flat tax on personal income, the lowest in Eastern Europe. According to Rabushka, it slashed the size and weight of the code by about 95% and replaced a 4-rate system by a single 12% tax and a monthly deduction.

The 20% profit tax rate remains, but social insurance was cut from 33% to 20%, VAT from 20% to 18% and dividends and interest payments taxed only once at 10% at the source of payment; people and companies who receive interest and dividends do not pay tax.[187]

185 'Flat tax offers Britain economic disaster', John Christensen and Richard Murphy, *Financial Times*, 15 September 2005
186 See Ernst & Young, country note on Ukraine; PricewaterhouseCoopers, op. cit.
187 'The Flat Tax Spreads to Georgia', Alvin Rabushka, RussianEconomy.org, 3 January 2005:
http://www.russianeconomy.org/comments/010305.html

Romania

Trajan Basecu's reform at the start of 2005 was welcomed by many top companies. Dacia, a car company that is part of France's Renault, said the move would give it more breathing space ahead of a major investment programme in 2005. GlaxoSmithKline, the pharmaceuticals giant, said the reform would help employees by increasing their disposable income.[188]

The tax cuts have so far proved to be a tremendous success. Corporate tax revenue in Romania exploded 21.1% in the first six months of 2005, refuting fears that the introduction of a 16% flat tax in January would lead to a collapse in revenues, in the short term at least. Tax receipts went up 17.3%. The health insurance fund saw additional receipts of 24.2%, while the unemployment fund also went up. VAT returns rose 27%.[189]

An earlier report said that the overall state budget revenue increased by 16.7% to 239,498.5bn lei in the first half of 2005 compared with the same period last year.[190] In the first half of 2004, revenue stood at 205,298.9bn lei. In real terms, the increase was 6.7%.

The sharpest rise in revenues was recorded in profit tax, even though the rate was slashed from 25% to 16%. The incomes derived stand at 35,587.9bn lei, up by 6,212.7bn lei from last year. One report said, referring to the profits tax: "Amounts collected outperformed estimates by 26.2%. The respective rise is also generated, to a certain extent, by micro-enterprises choosing to pay a profit tax rather than turnover tax this year".[191]

Despite the massive reductions in rates, income tax revenue dropped by a mere 1,696.2bn lei from the same period last year, a much better performance than hoped fro as recently as in early 2005. The former finance minister Ionut Popescu said at the time: "This proves that the introduction of the flat tax did not have bad effects".

Popescu said that introducing the flat tax had helped bring a part of the grey economy to the surface and raised the number of employees by 153,000 in the first quarter, helping to cut the jobless rate to a 13-year low of 5.5%.

However, Romania's success has been no thanks to the IMF, which has wreaked havoc with the country's finances and has constantly nagged the government to put up taxes. It has long demanded a hike in VAT to compensate for what it was convinced would be a large shortfall in revenues.

On 29 June, Romania's government approved an IMF-agreed budget review, setting this year's deficit ceiling at 0.74% of GDP.[192] But Romania, which had by global

---

188 'Romania economy: Will the tax changes fall flat?', Economist Intelligence Unit, 13 January 2005:
    http://www.viewswire.com/index.asp?layout=display_print&doc_id=1387942138
189 'Corporate Tax Returns in Romania Up 21% in H1 After Introduction of Flat Tax', Valerie Talacko, Global Insight, 10 August 2005
190 'State budget revenue increases by over 16% in first half of 2005', Rompres, 7 July 2005
191 Rompres, 8 July 2005
192 Reuters, 29 June 2005

standards a tiny budget deficit of 1.2% of GDP last year and originally forecast an equally negligible shortfall of 1.5% in 2005, has been constantly under pressure from the IMF to cut its deficit even further. It agreed with a visiting IMF team last June to cut the gap to below 0.75%; "this year's deficit would be of around 20.8 trillion lei or about 0.74 percent of GDP," Popescu said at the time. Opponents of a flat tax which cite Romania's supposedly problematic budget deficit need to understand the country's true position.

The IMF's problem seems to be that the tax cuts were too successful, fuelling buoyant domestic demand and threatening inflation and current account targets. However, spending restraints and perhaps higher interest rates could easily have done the trick. There have already been some silly and counter-productive tax hikes. On 4 June, the government hiked from one to ten percent taxes on gains from interests, deposits and other savings instruments and from the sale of real estate assets owned for less than three years, to the business community's discontent. The plan is that from 1 January 2006 the taxes on gains from interest, capital market transactions and sale of real estate assets held for less than three years will be increased to 16%.[193] There is also a lot of pressure for a rise of up to 3 percentage points in VAT to 22% but also some debate as to whether payroll taxes should be cut. As the figures show, however, no tax hike is necessary. But the result of the IMF's constant criticism was that Prime Minister Calin Tariceanu sacked Finance Minister Ionut Popescu, blaming him for the VAT hike proposal, and replacing him by Sebastian Vladescu, an economist with previous ministerial experience who has occupied senior positions in the Romanian oil industry.

As in most other countries, the government also operates various taxes on property. VAT is charged at 19% though there are lower-rated exceptions taxed at 9% or 0%. And as usual in Eastern Europe, payroll taxes remain too high. Employee have to pay social Security contributions worth 9.5% of their monthly gross salary; a health fund contribution of 6.5% and an unemployment fund contribution of 1%.[194]

Social security charges on employers are a massive 22% of the gross salary fund. There is also a 7% health contribution, 3% for the unemployment fund, and a 0.5-4% work accident insurance.

Other reformers: Poland

Jaroslaw Kaczynski's national conservative Law and Justice (PiS) party came out ahead of Jan Rokita's liberal conservative Civic Platform (PO) at the recent Polish elections. The PiS ran television broadcasts claiming that too much power in the hands of its coalition partners would reduce the food on Polish tables, a nonsensical proposition which apparently nevertheless influenced some Poles. This means that, unfortunately, a proper flat tax has been at least temporarily kicked into the long grass in Poland.

Nevertheless, it remains worth highlighting that the original proposal was known as

---

193 Rompres, 8 July 2005
194 See PricewaterhouseCoopers, op. cit.

the "3 times 15 plan": it would introduce a 15% flat personal income tax, 15% corporate income tax, and 15% VAT. The current 19%, 30% and 40% personal income tax brackets with many exemptions would be wiped away, as would the current 19% corporate profit tax. The proposed 15% VAT rate would imply unification from 22% for most goods. The Civic Party had calculated that total tax revenues under their plan would be roughly the same as now.

Germany

While this proposal doesn't directly concern the British debate, it has been extensively cited in the UK media so it is worth highlighting some of its features in this section. Kirchhof, an independent German academic, came to prominence in Germany in August and September 2005, during the general election campaign, as one of Merkel's key advisers.[195] Kirchhof has worked out that the German income tax code includes 418 exemptions and he has proposed an alternative, flatter code to replace it, as illustrated in the graphic.

His plan is not really a flat tax because it includes a 15% tax on incomes from E8,000-13,000 (the tax-free bottom level presently runs to E7,235); 20% on incomes from E13,000-18,000, and 25% on everything above E18,000.

FIGURE 17: GERMANY'S 2005 ELECTION TAX DEBATE

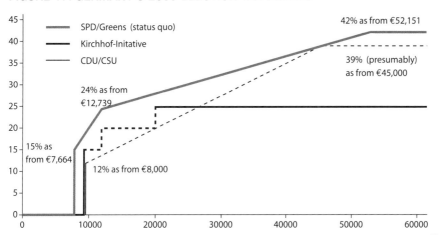

Note: Dotted lines indicate that a final has not yet been made in the specific tax bracket. Source: Barclays Capital [196]

Kazakhstan

The government cut the top rate of income tax from 30% to 20% on 1 January 2004, but there remains a graduated income tax regime from 5% upwards.[197]

195 For information on Kirchhof see www.uni-heidelberg.de/institute/fak2/kirchhof/ProfKirchhof.htm
196 Boone, Barclays Capital, op. cit.
197 Flat tax rate, *Directional Economics* June 2004, ING, London.

Chapter VII: Proposals for a British flat tax

Transitional Challenges

Opponents of a UK flat tax often claim that it would be harder to introduce in 'complex' economies than in the 'simpler' Eastern European economies. They are half-right in that several important features of the UK tax system would make it quite tricky to introduce a flat tax – but none has anything to do with the UK being a supposedly more advanced or richer economy. Would-be tax reformers everywhere should bear the following observations in mind:

- The lower the tax to GDP and public spending to GDP ratio, the better for tax reformers. This is bad news for the UK, where these two variables have been moving in the wrong direction.
- The greater the number of loopholes in the current tax system, the easier it is arithmetically to introduce a low-rate flat tax by sweeping them away—but the greater the political obstacles. In the UK, many former loopholes such as tax relief on mortgage payment have long since been swept away, making it arithmetically harder to move to a flat tax – but there is no entrenched resistance to change, as there is in the US with mortgage interest deductions.
- The greater the reliance on indirect taxation and taxes other than income and profits, the better. Again, this is not especially good news for the UK, which relies extensively on direct taxation.
- A system where some classes of people face radically different tax rates by virtue of arbitrary criteria such as age or geographical location is harder to replace by a flat tax. Yet again, this is a problem for the UK: pensioners are exempt from national insurance contributions.
- In most countries, the separate social security tax system should be incorporated into mainstream taxes and included in any flat tax reform. The fact that they have been unable to do so has been the great failure of the Eastern European tax reformers. In the case of the UK, employee national insurance contributions will have to be merged into a new tax on personal income.
- Another related point is that the fewer people that need to pay more tax from the introduction of a flat tax, the better. This will be a great challenge for any UK reformer and suggests that only a gradual approach will be politically feasible (because of the existence of the separate national insurance contributions tax); it also means that the tax to GDP ratio will have to be cut significantly in tandem with any move to a flat tax.
- Because of all the previous points, it is usually not possible simply to perform a static calculation of what the average income tax currently is (in the UK, 18.2%) and

to impose it as a flat tax on all individuals. The poor would end up paying more, as would most people on middle incomes. That is why the starting point of any calculation must be the current tax system, the standard rate (currently 22% income tax and 11% employees' national insurance contributions) and the current personal allowance.

• The better the state of the public finances before a reform is launched, the easier it would be to introduce major tax reform. This is because there would be inevitable short-term revenue losses and a temporary increase in borrowing when a flat tax is introduced, before supply-side effects kick in properly. Britain's national debt remains relatively low, facilitating reform (but it is burdened with huge unfunded pension liabilities), although its budget deficit is higher, making it harder.

• Tax systems are often closely integrated with benefits or social security systems. To avoid the benefits of radical tax reform being diluted, welfare reform ought to accompany tax reform. In the case of the UK, tax credits would have to be folded back into the benefits system, and all means-tested benefits and their interaction with income tax closely scrutinised to ensure that incentives to work and save are increased. Merely cutting taxes for some sections of the population may not increase incentives enough if the welfare system continues unchanged.

It is much easier for countries with a small state to introduce a flat and efficient tax code on Hall-Rabushka lines, as less money needs to be raised to keep current levels of spending funded. Because of Chancellor Gordon Brown's massive tax and spending increases of recent years, the introduction of a flat tax in the UK would now be considerably harder than it would have been in 1997 – but it remains possible and highly desirable as long as the reform takes place in parallel with a sustained freeze in public spending.

According to the most recent figures from the June 2005 OECD Economic Outlook, which have the advantage of being internationally comparable and politically neutral, public spending in the UK will have surged from 37.5% of GDP in 2000 to a predicted 44.5% this year and 44.8% next year. The gap between spending in the UK and the euro zone will have shrunk from 9.5 points of GDP five years ago to 3.5 points by next year.

The huge and growing size of the British state is the biggest single challenge for tax reformers. In theory, a flat tax of 44.8% would be required on all forms of income to pay for current levels of spending; this would mean a 44.8% tax on all earnings for work and all profits. The only way is for the government to hide as much of this tax burden as possible by using less visible taxes such as value added tax. Unlike in countries blessed with smaller governments, such as the US, Ireland, Australia or New Zealand, far more revenues would need to be raised to pay for existing government programs in Britain even with a flat tax. This is especially true when compared to the situation in the US, where tax reformers usually concentrate only on the federal government.

When economists and politicians talk of GDP, they are almost always referring to gross domestic product at market prices. But not only does this measure include the sum of all gross value added in the UK – by all accounts, the right measure of the tradeable part of the economy – it also includes the value of indirect taxes and subsidies. This is unfortunate as it implies a significant amount of double-counting and an artificial reduction in the size of the state and tax burden. It also makes international comparisons harder: countries that rely the most on indirect taxes and VAT, such as France, will look as if they are wealthier than countries that rely more on direct taxes, such as the US. International studies that attempt to measure the impact of the tax burden on economic growth will wrongly downplay the importance of tax as a barrier to growth.

The upshot of this discussion is that, unlike in the US, where it is quite easy (in pure economic terms, leaving politics to one side) to design a flat rate tax on income and profits that is both very low and immediately revenue neutral, without any need to cut or freeze public spending, it is simply not possible to do so in the UK. Radical reform to the British tax system will have to be accompanied by a downsizing of government as well as relying on significant supply-side effects to increase revenues.

It was easier to introduce flat taxes and massive cuts to direct taxation in Eastern Europe than it is in the West, because in Eastern Europe personal income tax and corporate income tax typically make up a smaller share of GDP and overall tax revenues. In the new member states personal income tax makes up 14.4% of total tax revenue, compared with a figure of 24.1% for the EU-15, according to an analysis of the OECD data by the Economist Intelligence Unit. The new member states also do not rely as much on corporation tax as do many other countries (these account for 6.6% of total receipts). The most important source of revenue for the government in the new member states are indirect taxes, which make up 38.7% of tax revenues, and social security contributions, which account for 38.8%.[198]

This does not make it impossible to introduce a flat tax in the West – and it would certainly be quite easy to do so for the US federal government, as demonstrated by Hall-Rabushka, Dick Armey, Steve Forbes and others – but certainly harder for the big spenders of Western Europe, including the UK. The challenges are greater in the short run, especially the process of transition.

According to the June 2005 OECD Economic Outlook, euro zone governments are expected to raise 45.7% of GDP in revenues this year, of which a little more than 40% of GDP will be through taxes. The UK is set to raise 41.6%, Poland 40.1%, while Scandinavian governments collect a whopping 58%. Outside Europe, the US government stands to raise 31.8% of GDP and the Japanese 31.2%. On that basis a flat tax would be much easier to introduce in the US (despite the existence of tax-deductible

198 Economist Intelligence Unit, op. cit

mortgage interest payments) and Japan.

The distribution of tax revenues between personal and corporate income taxes, value added tax and other forms of tax differs significantly across countries; this has a direct impact on how hard or easy it is to implement a flat tax. In Western Europe, personal income taxes amount to a relatively modest 9.2% of GDP, while Central Europe collects only 6.9% of GDP in personal income tax. However, in the United States, personal income tax are worth 12.5% of GDP.

Critics also wonder whether flat tax systems would have the same benefits in the mature and developed economies of Western Europe than they are having on the transitional economies of former communist countries. According to the Treasury, a flat tax may be seen as an attractive remedy for the administrative and economic challenges which are common to transition economies – but not for developed economies. But as we have seen in previous chapters, this is simply not true. The same challenges that plague Eastern Europe also exist in the West, even if they are usually less pronounced. While the size of the black economy in Russia and the extent of compliance problems were on a different scale, this does not mean that a flat tax would not herald great improvements in the West too.

Nigel Forman

The earliest available detailed proposal for a UK flat tax the author is aware of was published, somewhat surprisingly, by Demos, the left-wing think tank, in 1996. Its author, the then Tory MP for Carshalton and Wallington, Nigel Forman, lay out the case for radical reform and the introduction of a flat tax in a fascinating paper which had until now sadly disappeared without trace.[199] Unfortunately, none of its details remain applicable because the tax system, the level of spending and the entire economy have changed so dramatically since Labour was elected in 1997. Nevertheless, much of this paper remains interesting and could inform the current debate. It also contains interesting historical analyses.

His "preferred illustrative proposal" was to introduce a "single rate of 20% on all personal income whether from earnings, benefits or savings (which usually stem from retained earnings). Eliminate the current standard and higher rates of income tax. Eliminate all reliefs, exemptions and expenditures allowable against the tax, except for an indexed personal allowance of £5,000 transferable between spouses in the event that one of the married partners has insufficient income against which to set the allowance".

Equally fascinating is that, according to a Written Answer from the then Financial Secretary on 18 March 1996, the estimated revenue loss in the first full year at 1996–97 income levels would have been about £12bn or about one sixth of the total

---

199 Nigel Forman MP (1996), *Single Rate Tax: The path to real simplicity*, Demos: http://www.demos.co.uk/catalogue/singleratetax/

yield from Income Tax at the time.[200] Forman comments: "This official estimate of the aggregate revenue cost is based upon static, stylized assumptions which do not take into account what the Treasury itself describes as 'the substantial behavioural effects which might result from the introduction of such a change'. In other words, the initial cost of such a radical tax reform would undoubtedly be reduced (and possibly eliminated in due course) by the dynamic and positive effects which it could be expected to have upon economic behaviour and hence the flow of revenue to the Exchequer over a number of years".

The paper also cites figures provided by the Financial Secretary in a Written Answer on 26th February 1996, which argued that a revenue neutral package would require a single rate of tax of 23%, assuming a non-transferable personal allowance of £5000. Again, this is a static analysis from the Treasury. The paper also includes separate simulations by the Microsimulation Unit, Department of Applied Economics, University of Cambridge.

There is much else of interest in Forman's paper, including his proposals to reform the taxation of capital, abolish inheritance tax and introduce a lower rate of value added tax over a broader base (he admits this would require a change in EU law).

Adam Smith Institute

Moving on to 2005, the most influential detailed proposals in the UK have come from the Adam Smith Institute, a free-market think-tank. It has recently published two papers on the flat tax, The first, entitled "Flat Tax – The British Case" by Andrei Grecu[201], is largely a round-up of developments in Central Europe and despite its title doesn't get into details about the structure of a possible British flat tax. The second, most recent ASI publication in the subject is "A Flat Tax for the UK – A Practical Reality" by Richard Teather, associate senior lecturer in tax law at Bournemouth University and a consultant.[202]

In his ground-breaking study, Teather calls for a flat income tax of 22%, with a personal allowance of £12,000. The paper also discusses various options for raising the personal allowance; however, it does not address the vexed question of national insurance contributions or of business taxation. Nevertheless, rarely has a think-tank publication been this influential so quickly. Its arguments have been dissected by the UK Treasury, are well known among the Shadow Treasury team, have had an influence on some parts of the Liberal Democrats and were even adopted by several minor political parties, including Robert Kilroy-Silk's Veritas and a small Scottish party, at the May 2005 general election.

---

200 *Hansard*, 26 February 1996, Cols 371–2.
201 Grecu, op. cit.
202 "*A Flat Tax for the UK – A Practical Reality*" (2005), Richard Teather, Adam Smith Institute, http://www.adamsmith.org/pdf/flattaxuk.pdf.

Teather calculates that the poorest 10% of households would see their incomes increase by 9.2%, the next 10% by 7.9%, the third quartile from the bottom by 9.8% and the fourth by 12.1%, the biggest gain of any quartile. The top 10% would gain by only 1.4%. The plan would remove around 10m taxpayers from the income tax net.

Crucially, it would not be revenue-neutral, at least not in a static way: it would cut government revenues, before Laffer-style effects kick in and ensure that at least part of this reduction was compensated for by higher growth and reduced evasion.

This is the point on which objectors have pounced. The Treasury said: "Softening the impact of a flat tax on the poorest with a generous personal allowance is costly – in the case of the Adam Smith Institute proposal, £50bn a year."

Teather's reply, which is always ignored by his critics, is worth quoting: "A flat rate tax of 22%, with a tax-free personal allowance of £12,000, is possible. The initial loss of government revenue would be roughly £50bn per year, under 5% of GDP. When you take into account the potential £12bn of savings from abolishing minor tax reliefs, this comes to roughly the £35bn of administrative waste identified by the James Review. Even the £20,000 personal allowance is affordable if the £81bn of savings identified by the TaxPayers' Alliance could be realised".

It is important to note, however, that Teather's plan is probably the most limited version of a flat tax that it is possible to design. It would retain several important loopholes, including tax relief on charities and most importantly on pensions, and it would do nothing about capital gains tax or inheritance tax. As the Treasury put it: "Even the Adam Smith Institute proposals retain some deductions like charitable giving and pensions, which compromises the objectives of a flat tax".[203]

While the author suggests that the plan could also be extended to company tax in the final paragraph of his paper, he doesn't quantify this. Most importantly of all, Teather's plan leaves national insurance contributions entirely as they are at present. So even though his plan is presented as a 22% flat tax, most people would still be paying around a third of their income in direct tax.

Two other points made in Teather's paper regarding his analysis of the Treasury's ready reckoners, which are intended to give a rough guide to the reduction or increase in revenue from changes in tax rates, are most valuable. The first is that there will be some overlap between the revenue gains from abolishing reliefs and the cost of increasing the personal allowance and scrapping the higher rate; abolishing these reliefs along with implementing the flat tax may not therefore save the full current "cost" of the reliefs. The second is that the static revenue reductions from abolishing the top rate of tax are not as great as first expected because increasing the personal allowance takes people out of the higher rate band. Abolishing the higher rate tax on its own would initially reduce tax revenues by roughly £20bn a year, Teather says.

---

203 Documents released under Freedom of Information, op. cit.

John Chown

John Chown, a veteran tax and economic analyst and co-chairman of Chown Dewhurst LLP, recently penned his own analysis of a flat tax in a paper published by the Policy Institute, a think-tank in Edinburgh.[204]

The most interesting feature of Chown's plan is that it merges income tax and national insurance contributions for employees and employers into one integrated system. The proposal also addresses the thorny issue of integrating taxes on savings and dividend income into a comprehensive system.

Chown argues that as a starting point, a flat tax would involve eliminating the higher rate of tax, reducing the 10% band to zero (thus effectively hiking the personal allowance) and incorporating National Insurance contributions into an overall tax on income.

Somewhat surprisingly, however, he finds that "based crudely on current income tax and National Insurance receipts a flat tax rate of 44% would raise the same revenue as is currently received by HM Treasury from these sources". In addition, the personal allowance would increase by £2,090.

Chown deviates in important respects from every other proponent of a flat tax when it comes to taking into account dynamic effects before setting lower tax rates. He claims that "it would be futile to try to guess this benign effect in advance, and unwise to set a rate which assumed higher revenue". This constraint – in effect, he thinks it is too risky to assume dynamic revenue effects in the short term, even though he believes some such gains will materialise – means that his overall tax rate remains extremely high – and unfortunately it means that he is unable to make the main arguments in favour of the flat tax.

However, he does argue that "it is probably safe to assume that, after a couple of years, the flat tax rate could be lowered" but only very marginally. He assumes that cost savings together with higher yields from the better off will generate only an extra £10bn, though this figure is not derived from any formal model of the UK economy. This allows him to cut the flat tax to 42% after 2 years.

It is important to remember that under Chown's plans, companies would pay zero national insurance contributions – though their wages would have to remain the same as they are now, because the share currently taken up by employers NICs would be paid by employees as part of their overall wage tax.

A tricky problem for the model is how to treat investment and dividend income. Ideally, the author would like to charge the same 44% (or 42%) rate on these forms of income but because capital is far more mobile than labour, he realises that much would quickly leave the country. He notes that "lower rates obviously already apply, in the sense that National Insurance contributions are not applied to such earnings" and argues

---

204 Chown, op. cit.

for an explicitly lower investment and dividend income tax rate. Setting these rates at 22% would require an additional 1.5% on the new income tax rate.

However, by operating such a two-tier system taxpayers would have an incentive to cut back on salaries and try to classify as much as their income as possible as investment income. One solution, Chown argues, is to adopt an Estonian style corporation tax system whereby profits that are reinvested suffer no tax but distributed profits are taxed. He believes that such a reform could prove very attractive to investors and would allow the government to put up taxes on investment to the 40-odd percent he wants to charge on all income to create a comprehensive system. Current receipts from corporation tax outweigh those from investment and dividend income by more than £20bn; this means that similar savings would have to be found to pay for the change, Chown says.

Chown's research contains much that is extremely useful; unfortunately, because he refuses to include sufficient dynamic effects on growth and tax revenues, he falls in the same trap as the Treasury and other critics of the flat tax.

Howard Scott

Another detailed blueprint for a flat tax in Britain has recently been developed by Howard Scott, a Fellow of the Institute of Taxation and a retired tax partner with BDO Stoy Hayward.[205] It is probably the most detailed plan yet to be produced in the UK and goes much further than the Adam Smith Institute's proposals.

Under Scott's plan, which hasn't been published but which was summarised in an in-depth story in *The Business*[206], a 10% flat rate of tax would be applicable to all income and profits without exception, even doing away with personal allowances, as well as on all sales of assets for a price higher than they were bought for, with no allowance for consumer price inflation. The 10% rate would also apply to inheritance tax, value added tax and capital gains tax. It would be complemented by a further 5% social security tax payable on all earned personal income (which means that even under a plan as radical as Scott's, the overall tax rate would not be entirely flat). The only parts of the tax system that would remain outside the flat tax are excise duty, council tax, fuel tax, business rates and customs duties. Scott says: "People in the UK have been talking about a flat income tax rate of 25% with a large personal allowance, say £10,000. This would not work. The psychologically crucial figure is 10% and if the pass is sold on this, all is lost. We are talking about a substantial widening of the tax base but taxing it at a nugatory rate."

Although the proposal is more radical than almost every other flat tax scheme ever designed, it demolishes a central claim in the Treasury document released under

---

205 Copies of the full proposal are available from howard.scott@talktalk.net
206 'A 10% flat tax for Britain', Allister Heath, *The Business*, 14 August 2005

the freedom of information legislation, which said that "such a system is tough on the low paid unless you spend a lot of money on generous personal allowances or a very low rate of tax". But Scott finds that under his plan a "Mr Average" on £25,000 a year would be better off by over £100 a month, after all effects are accounted for.

The report assumes that 90% of the current levels of taxation need to be raised, equivalent to £438bn for 2005-06; his plan assumes tax cuts of £49bn from the amount forecast in Brown's 2005 Budget and a similar budget deficit. Of course, this need not be so: a supporter of the Scott plan could argue that much of this difference would be made up through positive supply-side effects, including faster economic growth.

Under Scott's proposal, income tax would be charged at 10% but with no personal allowances, no relief for pension contributions and no 25% tax free lump sum from a pension on retirement (the lump sum would still be available but taxed at 10%). Pensions paid out would only suffer 10% tax. However, all income tax breaks on share option schemes, enterprise investment schemes, venture capital trusts, individual savings accounts and other similar schemes would be removed. Lump sum redundancy payments (currently partly untaxed) would be hit at 10%, as would lottery winnings, premium bond prizes and National Savings interest. The income and gains of pension funds and charities which are currently tax free would suffer 10% tax. There would be no personal tax deduction for charitable donations.

Corporation tax would be charged at 10% on the GAAP-determined book profit of companies regardless of size, with no tax credits for research and development, no relief for employer pension contributions and no capital allowances. There would be no imputation credit against personal income tax on dividends.

Capital Gains Tax would be charged at 10% with no annual exempt amount, no indexation allowance, no taper relief and no loopholes. Most radically of all, gains on principal homes would be included, without indexation relief either on sale or on death. Inheritance tax would be radically reformed. Under Scott's proposal, estates would suffer 10% tax on the entire estate and an effective lifetime gifts tax would also apply, with no reliefs. Value added tax would be slashed to 10% but extended to all goods and services, with no exceptions. For good measure, the plan also includes a halving of council tax and stamp duty.

Before any dynamic or supply-side effects are included, there would be a £16bn shortfall compared with the revenue target, which may mean that vehicle excise duties, fuel and spirit duties or business rates may have to be hiked – but hopefully this wouldn't be necessary as the adoption of Scott would trigger an economic boom.

Scott's detailed calculations show that someone on £25,000 would be £200 better off a year before the effects of higher VAT on food kick in, entirely thanks to lower income tax and national insurance contributions, even after the abolition of the personal allowance. Even if this individual spent £10,000 a year on previously zero or low-rated VAT items, he would still be at least £100 a month better off.

Even people on £15,000 a year would be better off.

If there were a choice between the current tax system and Scott's proposal, many would argue without hesitation for the latter, which would sweep away the atrocious complication and distortions of the modern British tax system – and herald a dramatic improvement in incentives to work. However, the end result of Scott's ingenious model is far removed from the Rabushka-Hall flat tax model, which, as we have seen, is a consumption tax in all but name. One crucial feature of any rational tax system is that there should be no-double taxation. In Scott's plan, profits are first taxed at 10% at the level of the firm, then distributed profits are taxed again at 10%. Income is taxed at 15% (the combined income and national insurance contributions rate) and then again at 10% when the worker dies (through inheritance tax).

This is a drawback; another is that it cuts direct and indirect taxes but increases taxes on capital. Reducing direct taxes is a very good thing; but cutting consumption taxes shouldn't be a priority. Increasing taxes on capital should be avoided almost at any cost, even though under this scheme the damage from the increase in yield from those taxes is partly compensated by the very low marginal tax rate. Economic growth is determined by increases in the supply or productivity of labour and capital; to tax capital is to consume it (and hence destroy it) because governments invariably spend almost all their tax revenues on providing or paying for consumption goods or services.

Patrick Minford

Patrick Minford, the Cardiff Business School economist, has produced two main publications on the subject. In the first, an undated publication from Conservative Way Forward he makes three main arguments in favour of the flat tax.[207] In the second, published by Liverpool Macroeconomic Research, he takes the argument further.[208]

Minford calculates that the tax system produces a top marginal tax rate of about 60%, when all taxes and national insurance contributions, including consumption taxes, are included. For the average worker it is about 43%, he says; this is higher than the average tax rate of the economy.

Minford lauds the Ramsey Principle of equalising tax across groups, commodities and time, which he thinks should ideally apply; at the moment, the state is driving a bigger and bigger wedge between what things are worth in the market (such as labour) and the net-of-tax return to the people producing them (their wage, after tax).

Minford argues that a neutral tax system allows each activity in the economy to expand to the point at which each extra pound of value produced offers the same extra benefit to consumers. By contrast, in a non-neutral tax system, relatively subsidised activities expand beyond that point while the heavily taxed activity contracts inside that

207 'Is it Time for a Flat Rate Tax?', Patrick Minford, Conservative Way Forward; http://www.conwayfor.org/forward/ff1is.htm
208 'Agenda for a reforming government', Patrick Minford, Liverpool Macroeconomic Research and Cardiff Business School.

point. Minford says: "A worker on 40% marginal rate reduces his efforts more than a worker on a 20% marginal rate. The result is that the value to the employer of extra work worth one pound net of tax is greater for the 40% taxed worker than for the 20% taxed worker. It therefore pays to expand the work of the 40% group and contract that of the 20% group. This process should continue until the tax rates are the same".

This point is further strengthened by the fact that the elasticities of higher paid workers are higher than those of lower-paid workers, which increases the economic waste from the graduated tax system. Minford says that the reduction in the 60% tax rate to 40% in the 1980s led to higher revenues from these workers. The 40% rate abolition may therefore also largely pay for itself, he says. Minford says: "The share of income tax revenue paid by top earners was rapidly restored to where it had been and then went higher still, suggesting that the tax cut not only cost nothing at all but also may have even boosted overall revenues".

Finally, there is tax 'avoision', a term first coined by the Institute of Economic Affairs in the 1970s. This is most practiced by top-tax payers and lower rates would reduce that, which means that the reduction of revenues from tax rate cuts would be further reduced.

There are two main indirect or dynamic effects from tax cuts, Minford argues in his second paper. These two effects are often conflated by other economists (as they are in the rest of this report).

First there is what Minford calls the Laffer effects, net revenue recovery or back flow. Drawing on earlier work[209], he says that the response to the top tax rate of higher earners' labour supply is approximately 1% for every 1% cut in the top marginal rate – according to the evidence of the 1980s. Further down the income distribution the proportional response is about 0.5%. Cutting the top overall marginal tax rate by 10% would cause a net loss of revenue of only half the 'direct' amount, Minford calculates.

There is also a second effect from the tax cuts. The rate of economic growth rises by a third of the cut in marginal tax rates. A 10% average reduction in the average marginal tax rate across the economy (for example, from 40% to 36%) would boost the growth rate by 4% (for example, from 2.5% to 2.6%).

Minford's next step is to present an economically rigorous formula describing how government spending should be balanced with tax receipts over time. It says that the present value of taxes equals the present value of spending plus debt, all as fractions of GDP, which is a brilliantly simple way of looking at the problem. He then plugs in values close to those for the current UK economy, including for interest rates, trend growth rate, tax rates and public spending. In a remarkable display of the power of supply-side economics, he finds that a 10% reduction in the marginal economy-wide tax rate, as explained above, leading to an increase in growth of around 0.1 points a year,

---

209 Minford and Ashton, 1991, op. cit.

would allow massive tax cuts today while keeping constant the expected net present value of tax receipts. He finds that the tax burden could fall today by 6 percentage points of GDP – or more than £60bn – while still generating the same amount of tax revenue over time, thanks to the faster growth, and hence allowing exactly the same amount of spending. Minford writes:

> *"The average tax rate as a proportion of GDP can now fall, without reducing planned government programmes at all... Such a 6% of GDP drop in tax revenues is no less than £60bn per year! One can think of this as the permissible initial deficit after the tax cut; by implication this will be whittled away by growth until eventually the higher revenues would be sufficient to keep the debt/GDP ratio steady again. Now of course one might well wish to be more cautious than this but the point remains that there is substantial scope to run deficits prudently in the context of cuts in marginal tax rates".*

What would happen if the top rate of income tax were slashed to 22% and aligned with the standard rate? Minford agrees that there would be an immediate revenue loss but points out that over time Laffer effects discussed earlier are likely to recover much of this loss – especially given that top rate taxpayers respond the most to improved incentives.

Top rate taxpayers contributed 55% of total income tax revenue and 37% of income in 2005-6, Minford points out, which means that the income-weighted average marginal tax rate would fall by 12%, boosting growth by about 0.1 points a year. The static revenue loss from the ready reckoners would be a mere 2 points of GDP; any drop in tax receipts in the short-term would thus easily be covered as Minford's equation showed that receipts could fall by three times more under these kinds of scenarios.

The Cornerstone Group

In a pamphlet published at the end of September 2005, the recently formed Cornerstone Group of Conservative MPs outlined some of their views on a range of issues, including education and welfare.[210] The chapter on taxation was written by Edward Leigh, MP, chairman of the Public Accounts Committee. Leigh calls for a flat tax of 22% with a personal allowance of £10,000.

He also calls for all loopholes to be swept away, saying that when tax rates are very high tax reliefs are very important to people, who understandably guard them jealously, but when tax rates are much lower, as in flat tax regimes, they have far less value. In the interests of spreading simplicity and transparency, they can therefore be removed.

---

210 'Being Conservative: a cornerstone of policies to revive Tory Britain', Cornerstone, September 2005: http://cornerstone.blogs.com/

His plan does not include reforming national insurance contributions, corporation tax or any other tax. He says that the tax cuts would reduce revenues on a static basis by £43bn but that this is only 4% of GDP.

As Leigh puts it:

"Above all we must spend less of the public's money. But we must have an exciting, credible and costed programme to do so. We need a headline figure – not just one or two pence off the basic rate of income tax, but a dramatic reduction...As I know only too well from my work as Chairman of the Public Accounts Committee, dramatic efficiency savings could be made in many government departments if only the will and the boldness to make them could be found. There are many layers of bureaucracy which could be stripped away".

He points out that the James Review found almost £35bn available through achievable savings and that the Taxpayers' Alliance thinks there could be as much as £81bn. The average of these two figures is £58bn, Leigh says, leaving £15bn in change.

Leigh argues that the real 'poor' – the poorest third of the population – currently have to hand over 9% of their hard-earned salary to the government; under his flat tax plan, they would be entirely free of that burden, he says. This would help release them from the poverty trap; and Britain could then bid farewell to the Chancellor's Byzantine nightmare of tax credits and means-tested benefits, he claims.

The Liberal Democrats' tax proposals

On 25 May 2005, Hansard reported (Column 735):

Mr. [Alex] Salmond, [SNP MP]: I believe in local income tax, but how does the hon. Gentleman reconcile the concept of a local income tax with the concept of a flat tax?

Dr. [Vince] Cable [Lib Dem]: Local income tax is a flat tax, so I cannot see the point of the intervention. Local income tax might be right or wrong, but it is certainly flat.

In their consultation document on tax reform, the Lib Dems describe a possible flat tax system, though they end up rejecting it.[211] Their model, which should be seen more as thought experiment than anything else, is a simple structure with a large tax allowance (say, £10,000), a flat tax rate of, say 25% - plus national insurance contributions of 11% on all incomes and local income tax of around 4%. Everyone would pay a (roughly) 40%

---

211 Liberal Democrats, op. cit.

marginal tax rate. The marginal rate would rise from the present on average incomes but for most of these tax payers there would be less tax paid since the tax is paid on a smaller part of their income, the Lib Dems argue.

The scheme would be roughly "cost neutral" if the basic rate were approximately 28%. Alternatively a flat tax could be financed by scrapping tax reliefs elsewhere, they say, though their thinking is static and does not appear to include any dynamic revenue effects.

The Lib Dems reject a flat tax: "There is a risk that a flat tax system with a large threshold, if it is to be roughly revenue neutral, will benefit those on low incomes and high incomes but result in increased marginal and (probably) average tax rates for some of those in between. This is plainly a very serious objection in distributional terms".

The Lib Dems also list some possible changes that could be made to the tax system, without necessarily endorsing them:

- The abolition of the lower 10p rate band, effectively reducing it to zero. This cuts marginal tax rates for people earning £4,895 to £7,000 and average tax rates for all taxpayers. The proposal lifts some 2.5 million people out of tax. The cost is an estimated £6bn but there would be savings from reduced tax credits, according to the research.

- Lift the tax threshold to the minimum wage level (£8,615). The "cost" is £23bn not including savings from reduced tax credits. If the 10% rate were abolished too - that is, tax starts at 22% - the "cost" falls to around £16bn excluding the gain from scrapping tax credits, according to the Lib Dems.

Reform's flat tax work

Reform, the free-market think-tank, has also produced some work on the flat tax, first in an article by its former director Nick Herbert, now a Tory MP, and then in a more developed version in articles for the Financial Times and in Reform's magazine by Corin Taylor, the group's economic research officer.[212] The group has also published an analysis of the flat tax debate and is shortly due to release a series of briefing papers on the impact of the flat tax reforms in Eastern Europe.[213]

Taylor points out that had the Treasury chosen to increase public spending at the economy's trend rate of growth between 1999-2000 and 2007-08 – and thus not embarked upon Brown's absurd and dangerous spending binge – total spending would have increased to £470bn a year, saving £67bn annually that could have been used to slash taxes and

212 'UK has missed chance of dividend', Corin Taylor, *Financial Times*, 29 Aug 2005:
   http://www.reform.co.uk/website/pressroom/articles.aspx?o=106; 'Real Prudence', Corin Taylor, *Reform Journal*, September 2005:
   http://www.reform.co.uk/filestore/pdf/Corin%20Taylor.pdf
213 Reform Bulletin, op. cit.

transform the British economy. Such savings would have been more than enough to implement a flat income tax of 17% in Britain by 2008, Taylor says (this leaves national insurance contributions untouched). Using the Treasury's tax ready-reckoner, he finds that the starting rate of income tax can be abolished for about £7.5bn; the basic rate can be cut to 17% for £20bn; and the top rate can be reduced to 17% for £35bn. This would still have left £4.5bn, which could have been used to cut corporation tax by 3 percentage points, he says.

In its Bulletin on the flat tax, Reform also argued that the Treasury's main argument against the flat tax – that it would "cost a lot of money" due to reduction in rates and a likely increase in the income tax threshold to help lower earners – is disingenuous. Brown is already in the process of spending "a lot of money" in the form of a massive increase in public spending increases above the rate of economic growth between 1999-00 and 2007-08.[214]

In his earlier article for The Spectator, Herbert argued that if the next government were to restrain public spending growth to two percentage points below the trend growth rate of the economy (he estimates this at 2.75%), £40bn of annual revenue would be available for tax reductions by the end of the parliament without a penny actually being cut from services. He said that this "would get us halfway to a 20p flat tax rate with the starting rate, higher rate and all employee national insurance abolished".[215]

Reform has also commissioned the first focus groups and polls to gauge the extent of public support for the flat tax. The focus groups, produced by ICM, showed that even after being explained the difference between marginal and average tax rates, some people still couldn't fully grasp the difference between the two concepts. Reform highlighted a flat tax system whereby every taxpayer in the UK would pay less in income tax but there would be a deficit of £60bn between what the government collects under the existing tax scheme and what it would collect in the new flat tax. The focus group conclusions note that "the overwhelming feeling was that the UK should 'wait and see' if other countries, particularly western democracies, implemented the system and only follow their lead if it worked".

In a related poll, ICM also discovered that 50% of the population agrees that cutting the top rate of tax would make people work harder, against 43% who disagree. A majority of 51% to 35% agreed that if the top rate is lowered, the economy will grow faster. By a majority of 68% to 28%, people agree that a lower top rate of income tax will help to keep Britain competitive against other countries. The majority also thinks that the personal allowance should be lifted but it is clear that the public do not have a comprehensive understanding of the nuances of the tax code and average incomes.[216]

---

214 Reform Bulletin, op. cit
215 'A new deal for the poor', Nick Herbert, The Spectator, 17 March 2005:
    http://www.reform.co.uk/website/pressroom/articles.aspx?o=65
216 Tax Survey, Fieldwork September 28th-29th 2005, ICM,
    http://www.reform.co.uk/filestore/pdf/050930%20icm%20flat%20tax%20tables.pdf;
    Deliberative research: flat tax, a draft report of two focus groups in Shepperton, 27 September 2005, ICM,
    http://www.reform.co.uk/filestore/pdf/050930%20icm%20flat%20tax%20deliberative.pdf; Analysis by Reform:
    http://www.reform.co.uk/filestore/pdf/Reform-ICM%20flat%20tax%20poll%20analysis.pdf

Chapter VIII: Responding to the British critics

In its documents released under the Freedom of Information Act, the Treasury lists several major arguments against the Flat Tax. Before addressing these arguments, it is worth recalling a written answer on Wed, 15 June 2005 in response to a question by Vince Cable, the Liberal Democrat. This is what appears in Hansard:

> Dr. Cable: To ask the Chancellor of the Exchequer what studies his Department has conducted or commissioned about a 'flat tax' for (a) personal taxes and (b) business taxes; and if he will make a statement. [4535]

> Dawn Primarolo: The Government actively monitors the international developments in taxation, including the countries that have introduced 'flat tax' regimes. The Government have not conducted or commissioned studies on the introduction of a 'flat tax' in the UK.

It is a matter of semantics whether the documents released by the Treasury under the Freedom of Information Act constitute a "study" and it would be interesting to know when they were commissioned. The dates on the full version of the Treasury research include 28 July 2005 on one of its components, safely after the parliamentary question (and the overall document is dated 29 July 2005 on the Treasury website[217], but most of the other components that make up the Treasury disclosure are not dated.

The Treasury's secret papers

The following are quotes from the Treasury document, accompanied by a detailed rebuttal and occasional agreement.[218]

- *Flat taxes are "void of any progressive mechanism. Karl Marx's progressive tax structure was designed so that the tax burden was heaviest on those who were most able to contribute and lightest on those least able to contribute; the principle of wealth redistribution. Staggered rates of taxation are designed to achieve this principle".* It is interesting (and a little worrying) that the Treasury researcher openly appeals to Marx as a higher authority in this passage. It is equally strange that the Treasury confuses wealth redistribution with a graduated tax system. As any student of the tax system and of public economics should know, these two things are conceptually different. Tax and redistribution can be kept entirely separate. In a proportional tax system, someone who earns

---

217 See http://www.hm-treasury.gov.uk/about/information/foi_disclosures/foi_flattaxes.cfm
218 HM Treasury, op. cit.

10 times more than someone else also pays 10 times more in tax, which allows a huge amount of redistribution if that is what a government wishes to do. In any case, a flat tax with a zero rated personal allowance remains progressive in that the average tax rate increases with income, though it tends towards proportionality at very large incomes.

• *"The system of credits and exemptions, which work together with the bands, further encourages redistribution. Credits and exemptions allow governments to target minorities in society and take account of their individual characteristics, adapting their tax burden accordingly."* Later, the Treasury adds: *"countries such as the UK have introduced what are seen as complications like reliefs, deductions and allowances for specific reasons – often for reasons of equity, such as the Blind Person's Allowance or age related allowances".* It also adds: *"A flat tax like the Adam Smith Institute would remove a lot of the targeting and progressiveness from the current UK system".* The truth is that tax credits have been a complete disaster, as explained elsewhere in this book. They have utterly failed to deliver what they were supposed to achieve and have introduced huge additional complexity into the economy. Their biggest flaw is that they are set up in a way that guarantees they cannot work: receipts of tax credits are based on past (rather than present) income and circumstances, which almost guarantees that they will be inappropriate. A less damaging way of providing welfare payments to those whom a government wishes to target is to use the welfare system, rather than the tax system, and to assess people's circumstances on a monthly or quarterly basis, rather than according to their income during the previous tax year, as the tax credit system wrongly does. A properly designed flat tax system, like the one presented later in this book, would have a sufficiently large personal allowance to ensure that pensioners and the blind do not lose out. A larger personal allowance would also reduce the need for handouts.

• *"Furthermore, they can be designed to encourage or direct economic activity as the government sees best fit. This feature is wholly absent from the flat tax structure".* A government should avoid trying to influence the behaviour of its citizens through the tax system in a liberal society. A free-market economy is not compatible with politicians directing capital or effort in ways which they see fit, in the worryingly patronising words of the Treasury report; to think they do smacks of an authoritarian and dirigiste mindset. In any case, under a flat tax, economic growth, disposable incomes and asset values would grow much faster than under the present system. This would guarantee more money be given to charities without the need for the current huge tax incentives.

Pension provision is in meltdown in the UK, despite all the tax advantages. A more dynamic economy with lower taxes on income and capital, with freer citizens and companies, would provide a better framework for savings than the current failing system.

- *"Opponents therefore argue that a flat tax structure is beneficial to the rich and damaging for the poor. Proponents counter this claim arguing that even though the structure appears to be regressive, in reality, the lack of credits and exemptions and the increased transparency means that the rich in fact pay more than they do in even the top bands of progressive systems since practices of avoidance and exemptions and credit and exemption exploitation cease whilst the raised personal allowance protects the poor. (Again, this point is fiercely disputed since raw data to substantiate these claims is lacking.)"* The point made by the Treasury is partly right: those who gain the most from the loopholes in the current system are the better off. Under a flat tax, they would lose these advantages – venture capital trusts, for example, are almost exclusively the preserve of top rate taxpayers while the better off also gain far more from the current pension opt-out system. But proponents of the flat tax who claim that the rich would immediately pay more or a greater proportion of their income under a flat tax are generally wrong (some top-rate taxpayers would suffer net losses if their behaviour remained unchanged but most wouldn't), at least under most versions of a flat tax. At the moment, HMRC figures show that people on £100,000 or more pay average income tax of 33.4%[219]; under a flat tax of 28% (with a merged national insurance and income tax system), as proposed in the final chapter of this book, they would self-evidently pay a lower income tax share. Using different figures which look at original income and are derived from the ONS, the top decile currently pays 24.3% in income tax and national insurance contributions, under my flat tax system described in Chapter IX, they would pay only slightly less at 23.6% (crucially, though, while the average tax rate is not much lower, the marginal rate would be). It is true, however, that the better off under a flat tax would indeed eventually pay far more in tax than under the current graduated tax system – their taxable income would grow much faster, partly because of a reduced incentive to avoid taxes and partly because they would become more prosperous, work harder and take more risks. Given that supporters of a flat tax support a reduction in marginal tax rates and argue for improved incentives, it would be perverse for them also to call for higher tax rates on the rich.

- *Another problem is the supposed "ephemeral behavioural impact of flat tax*

---

219 Table 2.5, Income tax liabilities by income tax range, 2005-06, HMRC, http://www.hmrc.gov.uk/stats/income_tax/table2-5.pdf

structures and the permanent loss of tax as a tool to change behaviour and address market failures. In a flat tax structure the incentives are felt sharply when the structure is introduced hence why a mini-economic boom is often associated with the introduction of the flat tax structure. These incentives then begin to wear thin over time or even run out since there are only two levers (the rate and the personal allowance) which the government can adjust and these are strongly limited by public preferences on income redistribution and size of the public sector. Thus once the optimum lever levels are reached, no additional behavioural incentives can be easily added through the tax structure". This statement is based on an extremely dubious view of economic activity; paradoxically, it displays a quasi-Keynesian understanding of the supply-side economy which assumes that only changes in tax rates, as opposed to tax rates themselves, are what influences economic behaviour. The Treasury provides no evidence for this. It is also astonishing that the Treasury can claim that flat taxes are "often" associated with "mini-economic booms" when they are introduced, given that it spends much of the rest of the paper claiming that there is no evidence to suggest that flat taxes work.

• *"Flat taxes are usually adopted as a package of reforms and the effects cannot be unambiguously attributed to the actual flat tax".* This is true of all public policies; however, there is much theoretical and empirical work from economists which suggests that lower tax rates and a flat tax are good for the economy. The difficulty of identifying and quantifying the impact of one single variable does not prevent Brown from wrongly claiming – for example – that the drop in unemployment has been caused by his (in fact largely useless and very costly) New Deal. Professional economists use sophisticated econometric tech-niques to gauge the effect of a change in a single variable in a world of many, ever changing, variables. This is what is known as 'controlling for', 'keeping all else constant' or 'ceteris paribus'.

• *The Treasury highlights the "huge cost of introducing a flat tax (in this case £50bn). There is a serious lack of evidence that this could be made up through improved compliance and economic activity, as is suggested by proponents of flat taxes".* For a start, as argued in Chapter VII when analysing the ASI propos-als, this is a misinterpretation of Teather's claims. He also referred to various lists of reductions in public spending that he supports, all of which he deems to be wasteful spending, which would go a long way (and perhaps even the whole way) in plugging the alleged hole. In addition, nobody believes or argues that the whole of the £50bn would be recouped immediately. But the evidence is that the surge in growth, improved compliance and all the other effects would lead to a greater than commensurate surge in revenues very soon after the flat tax was introduced. When the Treasury talks of lack of evidence, what it really means is that it is not interested in the available evidence, including the highly successful supply-side tax cuts in the UK during the Thatcher era.

• *"To achieve the benefits of a flat tax all the current deductions, benefits and reliefs in the current system - often directed at the vulnerable - would have to be removed."* The Treasury specifically raises the issue of age related personal allowances, which provide a much more generous personal allowance for individuals aged over 65. This is a targeted measure that means nearly half of all pensioners do not pay income tax (and pensioners are also exempt from national insurance contributions). The age-related personal allowance is tapered away but pensioners continue to see a reduction in their tax bill up to £19,500. However, the Treasury is wrong to claim that "Many pensioners would face a tax increase under a flat tax unless the personal allowance was very generous – which would be unaffordable". By hiking the personal allowance and abolishing the starting rate of tax, all poor people would be significantly better off, making benefits and tax credits less useful; if calculated carefully, the increase in the personal allowance together with other changes would mean that no pensioner would be worse off under a flat tax (see the final Chapter of this book; unfortunately, it would also mean that a two-tier age-related system would have to continue for the time being, delaying the introduction of a fully comprehensive flat tax). Coming from the most profligate Treasury of modern times, claims of "unaffordability" should be taken with a bucket of salt. Assuming that the positive supply-side effects amounted to less than 100% of the value of the tax cuts, the Treasury is right to claim that less revenue would be raised under a flat tax; but from a free-market perspective this would in fact be a good thing, essential in helping to improve the UK economy's long-term competitiveness. However, tax credits are now so big that their abolition would require the creation of new benefits if the government wanted to ensure that no individual household (as opposed to income decile) be made worse off. Unfortunately, it would be wrong to claim that a personal allowance of £9,000 or even £15,000 would be enough to allow for the abolition of tax credits without making anybody worse off. (The issue of tax credits is really about welfare policy and of how best to help the poor get back on their own two feet. This is a topic too large to be tackled in this book).

• *"As the OECD has pointed out, just creating a single tax rate (even with increasing the personal allowance) will not deliver significant simplicity gains."* It adds: "Having a progressive rate schedule with a reasonably low number of* *income brackets is in itself probably not much more complex than having a single rate from an administrative point-of-view"*. The Treasury goes on to claim that "there would be less benefit from reducing 3 rates to 1 as in the UK compared with the reduction from 8 in Slovakia", which is trivially true. But this is not an adequate argument against the flat tax. As explained earlier, the aim is to dramatically simplify the entire tax code. It is also simply illogical to claim that because the UK tax code is (allegedly) less complex that those of Eastern Europe pre-reform, the UK should maintain its present system. This is part of an argument that many of the complexities in the tax system arise from the definition of the tax base and not from the rate structure itself, which is true (see the next section which discusses work from the Centre for Policy Studies and Cato Institute). But a drastic overhaul of the tax code, as proposed by Hall-Rabushka, would nevertheless lead to a vast reduction in the tax code. Individual taxpayers and companies would fill in a postcard sized tax form; even though there would still have to be more to the tax code than that, the economy would benefit immensely from the lower compliance and related costs of a Hall-Rabushka-style flat tax.

- *"Some countries with apparently 'flat rates' have really only made cosmetic changes - other taxes on income and/or complicated deductions mean that in reality they have neither low nor flat rates of tax on income. The flat tax is often combined with allowances, different taxes on different kinds of income and higher than normal rates of other taxes (Estonia has social security contributions of 33% and Hong Kong has high property taxes)."* For once, this is a good point and one which some supporters of moving to a flat tax in the UK have wrongly downplayed. The Treasury is right that there is as yet no pure flat tax in the world; but that is no reason not to move towards one. This is also a reason why this book advocates merging national insurance contributions with income tax. It is also worth repeating that in the original Hall and Rabushka model, the US social security system – which in theory is a self-funding system with an investment fund – is left untouched by the reform and continues to exist as before.

- *"Eastern European adopters also receive very little of their revenue from income tax so a flattening of the rates has a much lesser impact on total revenues than such a move would have in the UK."* This statement is also true. It confirms that it will prove harder to move to a flat tax in the UK – but that does not make it impossible or undesirable.

- *"In any tax system there is a trade off between efficiency and equity and differing economies use differing systems to achieve differing balances between the two".* The first interesting point is that the author (in common with all mainstream economists) acknowledges that the current tax system is distortionary and that it reduces economic efficiency. The second is that the Treasury paper assumes that equity is an objective concept – it is in fact deeply subjective. Often, people who claim this define "equity" as what they believe would (or should) be the outcome from a progressive system: someone who earns 10 times more than someone else should (they say) pay proportionally more (for example, 20 times more tax; in practice, of course, today's so-called progressive tax systems do not always work as advertised). But others may define equity as a system where someone who earns 10 times more should pay 10 times more tax; others may even see equity in a poll tax-style system. There is an overwhelming case for choosing the least damaging tax system because this is the one that would boost economic growth the most, allowing the overall size of the economic cake to grow the most and creating more opportunities for more people. There are many positive externalities to be had from living in a rich country, including access to the most advanced medical technology and high life expectancy; enlightened governments should stand aside and allow economies to fulfil their potential.

- *"Countries with transitional economies where collecting relatively small amounts of revenue from income tax (as a percentage of GDP) easily and reducing large shadow economies (or high avoidance rates) are a priority a very simple efficient system may seem most sensible. For countries with developed economies where there is a greater reliance on personal income tax and who use the system to achieve more objectives a more complicated but equitable system might be more appropriate".* Again, this does not follow. The shadow economy may not be as large in the UK as it is in some other countries but it remains huge nevertheless. It is also wrong to use the tax system for too many objectives; its sole raison d'etre is to raise revenues – and this should be done in the most painless way possible.

- *"Certain state benefits are tax-exempt – they would lose this and some benefits would be clawed back immediately through tax".* This is not true. There is no need to start taxing benefits from the government under a flat tax scheme.

- *"Personal savings such as Individual Savings Accounts and employee share schemes, both of which promote saving and investing".* The document also adds that *"removing the deduction for charitable contributions would reduce incentives to give. This is particularly important as wealthy donors who benefit the most from this deduction tend to favour hospital trusts and universities".*

Under a flat tax economic growth would surge. Even more significantly, the abolition of capital gains tax and the double taxation of dividends would lead to a surge in asset prices, boosting the national wealth. This would almost certainly swamp the negative effect of the abolition of incentives to charitable giving. A flat tax would also dramatically boost the return to savings and investing in shares while doing away with the bureaucracy of vehicles such as Isas.

- *"A true flat tax would eliminate taxation on savings and dividends. But this would give incentives to manipulate earnings to appear as interest of dividend income".* It adds that if *"dividends could be exempt (as they are already taxed at the corporate level), although this would increase the already large incentives for individuals to be remunerated in dividends".* There is a little truth in this and much misunderstanding. For a start, the question of people substituting dividends for salaries to cut their tax bills would only be applicable to small businesses and those where employees are also significant shareholders; it would not apply to ordinary members of the public who happen to be shareholders in companies for which they do not also work. It should be possible for the taxman to ensure that not too much money seeps out in wages disguised as income; under certain circumstances (such as employees paid ultra-low wages together with high dividends), dividends could be deemed equivalent to income. This would of course be bureaucratic and imperfect but would be better than preserving a version of the current system, which taxes profits twice. One of the central aims of the Hall-Rabushka work is to abolish the double taxation of income. As long as income generated by companies is taxed, for the Treasury to grab another chunk of the previously taxed income is obviously tantamount to double taxation. To remove the double taxation of dividends would lead to massive rise in share prices, which are usually valued through a discounted cash flow model. US share prices surged after the tax on dividends was slashed by the Bush administration to a rate that is much lower than that levied on most wages and salaries.

- *"Friedman et al (2000) found that high tax rates do not encourage the concealment of activity."* A similar point is made later in the paper by the Treasury, when it repeats the IMF's interpretation of the Russian reforms, pointing out that the *"flat tax has been only one part of a package of measures that are invariably introduced alongside a flat tax".* It also adds: *"one must also question the comparability of experience of these tax jurisdictions with the mature UK tax system and its established culture of compliance".* This research is noteworthy in being almost the only academic paper cited in the Treasury's analysis on the flat tax. But it is refuted comprehensively by the work of

Schneider, the world's prominent expert at measuring the size of the underground economy, who shows that high tax rates are a key explanation of tax evasion, as discussed extensively earlier in this book.

- *"Proponents of a flat tax have to face up to the reality that such a system is tough on the low paid unless you spend a lot of money on generous personal allowances or a very low rate of tax – or both".* First, a personal allowance is about people keeping more of their money, not the government 'spending' any of it. Second, the statement suggests that the author hasn't read any of the existing flat tax proposals, or else they would know that this point is made by all the authors.

- *"The IMF has indicated that there will be a revenue shortfall in Romania due to the flat tax despite VAT going up to 20% and excises being sharply increased."* A large enough tax cut will lead to a drop in revenues in the short-term; but the argument is that over a period of time tax revenues will bounce back. In any case, the alleged revenue shortfall in Romania is trivial as a share of GDP when compared to that facing Chancellor Gordon Brown in the UK. The IMF's attitude to the Romanian reforms has been grossly unfair.

- *"In 1999 the Norwegian Flat Tax Commission found that the first year effects of flat tax reform will give by far the largest tax cuts to high income individuals".* The answer to that can only be: so what? Every section of society would benefit from the increased growth and reduced compliance costs that a flat tax would bring about; that those who earn more will also gain more should be irrelevant.

- *"In the longer term, supporters of a low flat tax argue that increased compliance and economic activity deliver increased revenues – but the evidence is at best mixed. With regard to the Reagan era, the alternative view is that the tax cuts caused the increased US budget deficit of the 1980s".* But this so-called alternative view is simply not true, as shown elsewhere in this book. The Reagan deficit of the 1980s could entirely have been avoided had Congress reined in public spending.

- *"Heroic assumptions are made about economic gains which trickle down through the economy".* The mass of evidence presented in this book suggests that the assumptions are far from heroic; what is most heroic is the Treasury's ludicrous view that ever greater levels of public spending and tax are having no negative impact on economic performance.

- To the claim that Slovakia is an OECD member and not a developing economy, the Treasury says "it is not a reliable source of comparison with UK - the fourth largest economy in the world with a mature stable tax system". All economies, small and large, would gain from lower taxes. Of course, there are many differences between countries which need to be taken into account when designing a flat tax system for the UK. The Romanian experience remains of great interest to UK tax reformers.

- "There is very little evidence that flat taxes work. Flat taxes on income tax have only so far been used by countries where little revenue is generated from income tax (often due to difficulty in securing compliance) and combined with higher charges in other areas such as social security." The truth is that there is a huge amount of evidence, both empirical and theoretical, that cutting tax rates "works" in the sense that it boosts taxable income and increases economic growth. It is a terrible pity that the Treasury cannot acknowledge this.

Concerns about simplicity

The Centre for Policy Studies, a conservative think-tank, has published a paper by David Martin which argues that while lower and simpler taxes are immensely desirable, a flat tax is not the best means of achieving these objectives.[220]

While the paper includes some (not particularly novel) general arguments against the flat tax, which have already been addressed elsewhere in this book, its main contribution is to argue that a flat tax would not mean the repeal of most tax law.

Martin argues that abolishing reliefs would only represent a minimal reduction in the current huge volume of tax law, though he admits that there would be a noticeable impact on ordinary tax returns for many people. "It is doubtful that more than about 1% or 2% of current direct tax law would be repealed", he says.

He argues that tax law can be simplified – but that this has little or nothing to do with introducing a flat tax. At least half of all tax law could be hacked away but "there would, however, remain a nexus of provisions whose retention is probably justified". In these he includes matters such as group relief, whereby tax losses of one company in a group can be surrendered to eliminate profits of another company in the group; and roll-over relief, whereby capital gains on assets used in a business can be replaced without an immediate tax liability. Other structural rules will be required, he says. Companies do not pay tax on dividends received from other UK companies, to avoid double-taxation; but anti-avoidance rules would be needed to prevent the payment of interest tax free by disguising the interest as a dividend.

Martin has a point, even though he overstates his case and appears to be

---

220 David Martin (2005), *An overview of the flat tax*, Centre for Policy Studies: http://www.cps.org.uk/pdf/pub/415.pdf

unaware of the full radicalism of a comprehensive Hall-Rabushka model, which would do away with many more of the complexities of the tax code than he seems to realise. However, Martin's group relief example is spot on and the truth is that even under Rabushka-Hall some tax legislation would still be needed. However, the burden – especially on individuals – would be dramatically reduced.

A related point is made by Chris Edwards in a fascinating recent paper outlining different options for tax reform.[221] Some business tax items, such as transfer pricing, would continue to create complexity under Hall-Rabushka; the taxation of financial institutions would also need special rules. Edwards says: "Experts have pointed to areas where the flat tax would be vulnerable to business tax sheltering, such as transfer pricing that would require extra policing. Transfer pricing is the shifting of profits from high-tax to low-tax countries using the prices of products and intangibles that are traded between corporations and their subsidiaries. Another point of trouble for the flat tax would be separating financial and non-financial transactions".

Martin's main argument is reasonably close to another, which is that a lot of the complexity of the tax system is due to difficulties in defining income. A partner for a big accountancy firm was quoted as saying: "It won't really affect the industry. Accountants aren't employed to apply rate of tax to income; there are software programmes that do all that. Our job is to work out what the income is. Individuals and companies will still need us to do that, regardless of whether the tax applied to that income is graduated or flat".[222] Again, there is some truth in this statement, though it underestimates the radicalism of a pure Hall-Rabushka tax.

A Hall-Rabushka flat tax would not be a complete panacea in the sense that there would need to be more to the tax code than simply the two postcards which would be its visible face; crucially, however, the additional red tape would be hugely less than the present levels and most individuals would only need to think about the two tax forms, leaving what is left of the rest of the tax codes to a handful of big companies to worry about.

Lombard Street Research

This paper, which created a stir when it was published in early October 2005, argues that while a flat tax was feasible in the 1960s, it would now be politically suicidal.[223]

According to the authors, virtually all the potential gains have been exploited since then by the reduction in top rates, which were cut from 98% to 40% by Prime Minister Margaret Thatcher in the 1970s and 1980s, and the elimination of numerous reliefs, such as that which mortgage interest used to enjoy. Today, 50% of income tax

221 Chris Edwards (2005), *Options for Tax Reform*, Policy Analysis 536, Cato Institute: http://www.cato.org/pubs/pas/pa536.pdf
222 'Tax Flat rate - Tax: going flat out', *Accountancy*, 26 September 2005
223 'Fat chance: Flat tax - an idea whose time has gone', Brian Reading, with help from Charles Dumas, Lombard Street Research, *Monthly Economic Review 195*, September/October 2005.

is paid by 10% of top tax payers, which they appear to believe confirms their claim that Laffer-style effects have already run their course. Brian Reading, the paper's lead author, argues that "they would gain a lot from a flat rate while many others would lose". He adds: "This 10% (3m) would gain a lot and many (27m) would lose from the move to a flat rate. It would be political suicide".

This paper's conclusions are wrong but it includes much useful data and a good analysis of official tax data from HMRC, as well as some interesting facts. For example, Dumas points out that when Sir Robert Peel re-introduced income tax in 1842, it was at 7d in the pound, or just 2.9%, on incomes over £150 a year, equivalent to £635,000 a year at today's prices.

Another interesting fact is that when Reading was at the Conservative Research Department in the late 1960s, a tax panel worked on the implications of a flat tax for the UK. They calculated at what rate it should be, its yield, and losers and winners. Dumas wrote about it in an article in *The Economist* published some time between 1972 and 1974, making the case for a 15% flat tax, which was the average tax yield, for the UK – but the findings of the research have otherwise been completely forgotten. Not only did Edward Heath and the rest of the Tory party hierarchy refuse to implement the study's findings, they were so petrified by its implications that they decided to keep it a secret.

According to figures from HMRC cited by the authors, the average take from taxpayers' total income is 18.2%,[224] but about 90% of taxpayers pay less than this. They call an 18.2% flat tax the "revenue neutral" rate, which is their biggest mistake: it assumes that taxable income will remain the same under a flat tax – and that there will be no dynamic effects whatsoever.

---

224 HMRC, Income tax liabilities, by taxpayer's marginal rate, 2005-06, op. cit.

FIGURE 18: WHO PAYS HOW MUCH INCOME TAX

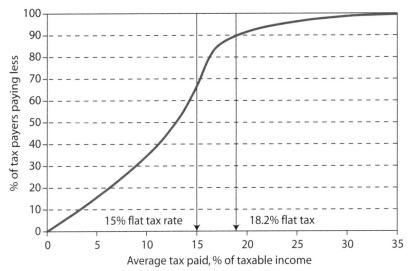

Source: Inland Revenue, Lombard Street Research

Because of the personal allowance, the flat tax rate would have to be set higher than 18.2% — they calculate that on a static basis to collect the same revenue as is collected now with a flat tax would mean an average rate of 23%. If all reliefs and allowances with the exception of the personal allowance were to be abolished, this could fall to 20% — but this would still leave 22m people worse off, they say.

Abandoning revenue neutrality – in the authors' misleadingly static, arithmetic definition of that term – would obviously reduce the number of losers. But it would "cost" £20bn to lower the tax rate to 18%. This would still leave 50% of all tax payers (15m) losing out; taking the personal allowance to £7,500 would take 3m out of the tax system but would still leave many losers.

However, they concede that the problem could partly be dealt with by merging income tax with national insurance contributions for employees and the self-employed. The average tax rate under the static assumptions would be 25%. Under this scheme, the big winners would gain less and there would be fewer and smaller losers. However, this would break down because national insurance contributions do not hit pensions.

According to Reading: "Only earned income (including earned self-employed income) is subject to NICs. Investment income is not liable (and nor are the earnings of those of us aged over 65 who continue to work). For any given personal income level, combined tax and NIC payments can vary widely. People on lower earned incomes can pay significantly more than people on higher investment incomes or pensions. NICs depend less on what you earn than who you are. Attempting to create a workable flat rate tax regime by consolidating NICs with income tax might reduce the gains on high incomes to the benefit of low incomes. But again the political arithmetic of losers and winners is impossible. The tax burden on pensioners would be significantly increased. Most pensioners would end up much worse off".

The Lombard Street calculations are accurate and useful, as far as they go. What they show is that under the erroneous assumption of zero supply-side effects and zero elasticity – or responsiveness – of taxable income to changes in after tax income on a marginal pound, the flat tax would run into deep problems. But this has long been the main argument of flat tax opponents.

Their most powerful point is that about national insurance contributions and the fact that pensioners would lose out from an amalgamation. Because of this feature of the UK tax code, any move to a flat tax will have to be gradual.

The Economist/PricewaterhouseCoopers

For a recent article, The Economist asked John Hawksworth, an economist at PricewaterhouseCoopers, the accountancy giant, to produce a basic quantification of what a flat tax would involve.[225] Crucially, the simulation only took income tax into account and didn't assume any dynamic effects; this assumption was used by PwC for the purposes of simplicity and not necessarily because it didn't agree that a flat tax would have dynamic effects. Using the back-of-the-envelope calculations requested from him by the newspaper, Hawksworth found that the current yield of income tax could be preserved with a flat rate of 30% and a personal allowance of £10,000. There would be losers as well as winners compared with current tax bills, as illustrated in the graphic.

Low earners and those on larger incomes would gain, while many in the middle would lose out. Someone on £10,000 would gain 8.7% of their income; someone on £100,000 would gain 5% of their income.

Losses peak at 3.5% of income at the current higher-rate threshold of £37,295. In all, more than 10m income-tax payers – a third of the present number – would lose from such a reform, the research found.

Different allowance sizes and tax rates would obviously generate different results. But under the static assumption made in this and similar research, a similar problem always emerges. "If you raise the same revenue but increase the allowance, then it is the people in the middle of the income tax paying population that lose from a flat tax," says Christopher Heady, head of tax policy at the OECD, quoted in The Economist and obviously assuming a static model of the world.

---

225 Hawksworth hasn't published the results. 'A dip in the middle', *The Economist*, 8 September 2005

FIGURE 19: A 30% FLAT TAX WITH STATIC ASSUMPTIONS

Flat tax*, gain or loss compared with today, £

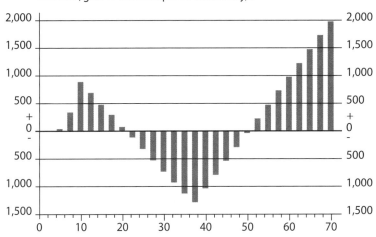

*£10,000 tax-free allowance, 30% rate on taxable income
Source: John Hawksworth, PricewaterhouseCoopers, The Economist

Prospect Magazine

A similar attack against the flat tax was made in a short diary article in the June 2005 issue of Prospect magazine, a thoughtful and open-minded monthly journal of the left. Advising Osborne, then the recently appointed Tory shadow chancellor, not to be tempted by the idea, it claimed that a flat tax in Britain would make most people worse off. [226]

"Today there are 30m British taxpayers. If the threshold was set at £10,000, around 13m would have no tax bill", the article argued. It added: "To raise, from the remaining 17m, the same amount of tax as was actually raised in 2004-05, the flat tax rate would need to be 31.5%. Apply this to incomes of varying sizes and you find those earning £0-20,000 and over £60,000 end up better off, while the 'hard-working families' on middling incomes lose out."

Replying on the Adam Smith Institute's blog, Dr Madsen Pirie, the think-tank's president, said: "The idea that tax revenues are fixed, and that if some pay less others must pay more, is about as sensible as the 'wealth is fixed' outlook. The point of flat tax is that it broadens the tax base. People avoid less, evade less and declare more. Then they earn more". [227]

226 'Bad idea for George Osborne', *Prospect*, June 2005:
    http://www.prospectmagazine.co.uk/article_details.php?id=6910&issue=506&category=153&author=&AuthKey=
    744f6c9eef940f980647af06dc8b6290
227 'Missing the point', Dr Madsen Pirie, *Adam Smith Institute Blog*, http://www.adamsmith.org/blog/archives/001319.php

Institute for Public Policy Research

The Institute for Public Policy Research, a left-wing think-tank, has emerged as the most vocal and articulate critic of the flat tax in the UK. The group has so far published two short articles on the subject.

The first, by Dominic Maxwell and Rachel O'Brien, was printed in the summer 2005 issue of their scholarly journal.[228] The article's motto is that "For every tax problem there is a solution which is straightforward, uncomplicated and wrong" – and that this, of course, applies to the case for the flat tax.

According to the authors, the case for the flat tax rests on two arguments:
1) simplification would reduce the costs of collection and compliance
2) rates that are both simpler and lower would actually increase revenue.

The authors argue that many of the allowances that exist in the current tax system are there for a good reason and are therefore desirable – although they agree that simplicity is an important feature of a tax system, they say that it is not the only one and that sometimes other objectives should take priority.

They also argue that the existence of multiple, graded tax bands is not the most complicated thing about the tax system. They say: "With the computerised nature of pay as you earn (PAYE), and online-self assessment systems being used to calculate most of the income tax paid in the UK, it is highly implausible that the existence of several rates imposes a high (let alone increasing) collection cost. If the technical sophistication exists to run the London Congestion Charge, then banded income taxes are surely not beyond our Ken".

They then go on to make the standard arguments about the theoretically ambiguous outcome of a tax cut, claiming that it is unclear whether or not the income or substitution effect would predominate. But the research presented in this book suggests that in practice the substitution effect does indeed predominate – and that reductions in marginal tax rates do indeed increase taxable income.

What they see as their 'killer fact' is that income taxes as a share of GDP in Estonia have dropped slightly from 8.2% of GDP in 1993, the year before the flat tax, to 7.2% in 2002, according to their paper. However, given the drastic reductions in tax rates under the flat tax, and the surge in economic growth in recent years, the fact that Estonia's income tax to GDP ratio has fallen so little should be seen as a vindication, rather than an indictment, of the pro-flat tax dynamic worldview.

In what is perhaps their most interesting point, the authors argue that the existence of a large personal allowance has implications for citizenship and the principle of reciprocity, pointing out that the debate would be different if large numbers of people pay no tax on their income. They are right about this; some US organisations with diametrically opposing views have made the same point. From a free-market

---

228 Dominic Maxwell and Rachel O'Brien, *Commentary*, Public Policy Research, Summer 2005.

perspective, that some people do not pay direct taxes at all would indeed make them more likely to support tax hikes on those that do; however, on balance, one can argue that it remains better for the poor to pay as little tax as possible to reduce the need for welfare spending.

The IPPR authors also criticise Teather's work at the Adam Smith Institute because he demonstrates that "the distribution of tax savings as a percentage of income, rather than in absolute terms" and "by combining the effects of a single tax rate with the effects of heavy tax cuts, the report gives only half the picture". They also claim that supporters of the flat tax neglect to assess the short- and long-term impacts that may arise from the proposed spending cuts, including on business tax credits for research and development. But whereas tax breaks for investment may indeed have a positive effect, these would be swamped by the far greater overall gains to be had from a flat tax.

In a separate short article for the New Statesman, Nick Pearce argues that the flat tax's main effect would be to attack the poor.[229] He argues that "simply smoothing the current, stepped rates of income tax to a single flat rate would disadvantage low earners and benefit the better off." This is standard anti-flat tax argument which assumes that the current average 18.2% tax rate would become everybody's marginal tax rate and would mean 90% or so of the population paying more tax. The point is that all of the flat tax proposals have been designed specifically to avoid this – and that is the reason why most are accompanied by proposals to reduce the overall tax burden, something which of course the IPPR does not support.

Pearce would much rather see the money allocated to tax cuts be spent by the state on his favourite programs. His main argument is that "public services are pro-poor in their distributional impact. Adding together the value of benefits in kind, including health and education, the amount received per person by the poorest 40% is twice that of the top 20%. That is why social injustice, not liberal prosperity, results from deep cuts to public services". However, flat taxers would argue that over time the best thing for the poor is to boost economic growth by as much as possible and that a flat tax would help achieve this. They would also argue that the massive increase in the reliance on the state is very damaging. Finally, if the main interest in public services is their impact on the poor and especially on income redistribution, then their logic actually implies that there is a case for making the better off and the middle classes pay for their own public services; that would massively boost the progressiveness of the welfare state and ensure that the amount received by the poorest 40% would be even greater than that of the top 20%.

Pearce then goes on to reject the argument that the tax cuts would pay for themselves, calling it voodoo economics (though he fails to point out that most advocates of a flat tax don't necessarily argue that all the tax cut would be recouped).

---

229 'Nick Pearce trounces the flat tax', Nick Pearce, *New Statesman*, 12 September 2005

He relies on the IMF paper on Russia and the decline in income tax as a share of GDP in Estonia to back this up and claims that the experience of the 1980s showed that the supply-side arguments failed.

Finally, he argues that computerisation and pay as you earn make the case for a flat tax weaker than at any previous time – though this is hardly the experience of the millions of taxpayers and companies who find the current tax system unacceptably complex and hard to understand.

Chapter IX: The Heath proposal

A step towards Hall-Rabushka

My proposal for the UK tax system goes as far as I believe to be feasible – in the short-term, and given political constraints, the current tax system and existing levels of public spending – towards the model designed by Hall-Rabushka. My plan aims for a flat rate of tax of 28% on individuals and companies, with no taxes on dividends, capital gains, inheritance and interest payments and a personal allowance of £9,000. Crucially, this flat tax plan includes national insurance contributions, which would be merged with income tax. There would be just one – albeit an important – exception to the single rate: pensioners would pay tax of just 22% on income above their new £9,000 personal allowance. This is because they are currently exempt from NICs; the 22% rate is to ensure that they do not lose out from my reform.

The proposals outlined in this chapter would be fiscally responsible because they would bee accompanied by a serious reduction in public spending growth, the elimination of some useless or wasteful government programmes and increased receipts from privatisation – and because the proposed 28% flat tax would give the economy a huge boost by unleashing incentives.

This chapter does not provide a complete blueprint and all the figures used are necessarily approximations and orders of magnitude. Additional work would need to be done to model the interaction between this flat tax proposal and a reformed welfare system. A more advanced proposal would also have to include data and information that is not currently in the public domain; all of this would have to be plugged into a comprehensive supply-side economic model of the UK economy. Further reforms would need to address important issues such as national insurance contributions for employers, stamp duty, council tax and the myriad other taxes that fell outside the scope of this study.

Perhaps most important of all, a flat tax rate of 28% remains far too high: the current plan should thus only be seen as the first phase of a move towards a fully comprehensive and low flat tax. My assumption in this study is that it is better to start moving in the right direction, albeit rather too modestly, rather than remaining stuck in a variant of the current damaging system through excessive ambition.

It is with these caveats therefore that I present a first draft of a first step towards a UK flat tax. Figure 20 illustrates how employees national insurance contributions and income tax currently interact for a typical employee; and how this would change under the proposal. The effect of tax credits and means-tested benefits are not included.

FIGURE 20: THE HEATH FLAT TAX

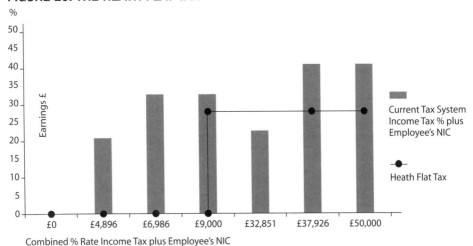

Combined % Rate Income Tax plus Employee's NIC

Earnings £	£0	£4,896	£6,986	£9,000	£32,851	£37,926	£50,000
Income Tax %	0%	10%	22%	22%	22%	40%	40%
Employee's NIC Rate	0%	11%	11%	11%	1%	1%	1%
Income Tax % plus Employee's NIC	**0%**	**21%**	**33%**	**33%**	**23%**	**41%**	**41%**
Heath Flat Tax	**0%**	**0%**	**0%**	**28%**	**28%**	**28%**	**28%**

The current UK tax system

In 2005-06 most taxpayers are liable on taxable income other than savings and dividend income as follows: 0% on the first £4,895, 10% per cent on the next £2,090, 22% on the next £30,310 and 40% above £37,295 a year.[230] In addition, they are faced with national insurance contributions of 11% on wages and salaries between £4,896 a year and £32,850, and at 1% on earnings above.[231] Employers pay 12.8% NICs for each employee on earnings above £4,896 a year (this is not shown here; I will be treating employers NIC as a separate tax on companies to be ignored under this first move towards a flat tax). Crucially, however, NICs are not paid by pensioners and do not cover other, non-wage or self-employed income; this is why my model has a 22% flat tax for pensioners earning over £9,000 a year.

Assuming that NICs start at the same rate as the starting rate of income tax (there is a small difference) and that employers NICs should be classified as a tax on the company rather than its employees – a contentious proposition economically but one

---

230 HMRC Rates and allowances 2005-06, Income Tax, http://www.hmrc.gov.uk/rates/it.htm
231 HMRC Rates and allowances 2005-06, National Insurance, http://www.hmrc.gov.uk/rates/nic.htm

with which most workers and employers intuitively agree – most employees in the UK face 5 rates of tax: 0%, 21%, 33%, 23% and 41%. This is shown in Figure 20.

Under the flat tax reforms proposed in this book, there would only be 2 rates: 0% and 28% (though pensioners would pay 0% or 22%, which is not shown on Figure 20). Marginal tax rates become lower for everybody on all income except for that between £32,850 and £37,925, where it increases from 23% to 28% (pensioners are exempt from this increase as they only pay 22%).

Proposed changes under the Heath flat tax

The following paragraphs examine in turn all the tax areas that would be radically reformed under this proposal. They begin by examining the tax system as it currently exists, describing tax rates and thresholds in 2005-06 and the revenues they generate for the Treasury. The proposal then goes on to suggest how these various taxes would be reformed and in some cases abolished completely – and the effect this would have on static government revenues.

Income tax

- Top rate of income tax

In 2005-06, the current 40% top rate of income tax is set to raise £42.6bn, according to HMRC.[232]   This is not the whole of the burden shouldered by higher-rate taxpayers: they also pay £732m under the starting tax rate and £22.5bn under the 22% basic rate.

Under my proposal, the top rate of income tax would be cut as a first step from its current 40% to 28% (and abolished entirely for pensioners). The impact of this on the Treasury would not be as large as many believe, even before dynamic effects are accounted for. It is important to understand that even abolishing the top rate altogether and bringing it in line with the 22% rate would reduce revenues by less than half of that £42.6bn (probably about £20.5bn) rather than the whole thing, as sometimes argued. In any event, under my proposal it would be cut by only 12 percentage points.

Changing the higher-rate by 1p cuts revenues by £1,140 on a static basis, according to the ready reckoners, the Treasury's rough guide to the impact on government revenues of changes in tax rates or thresholds.[233]   This means that the static revenue loss from my plan would be only £13.68bn, excluding the impact on pensioners. However, the ready reckoners assume an unchanged personal allowance when calculating the impact of a cut on the top rate. A simultaneous increase in the

232 HMRC, Table 2.6, Income tax liabilities, by taxpayer's marginal rate, 2005-06, http://www.hmrc.gov.uk/stats/income_tax/table2-6.pdf
233 HM Treasury, Tax Ready Reckoners, op. cit.

personal allowance – as per the present flat tax proposal – reduces the revenue loss suffered by the Treasury of a cut in the top rate. The result is that the ready reckoners' estimate is far too high; it includes some double counting with the revenue loss earmarked under an expansion of the personal allowance (see section below).

However, I have decided to stick with the £13.68bn figure. This is because my flat tax plan also assumes that pensioners would enjoy the complete abolition of the top rate of tax – they will face a 22% flat tax, unless the rest of the population. This would reduce government revenues by a few billion pounds a year. A plausible approximation is to assume that the £13.68bn figure includes both cutting the top rate for non-pensioner taxpayers to 28% and the additional revenue loss from abolishing the top tax rate altogether for pensioners.

- ## Starting rate

This is forecast to bring in around £5.8bn this year;[234] it would be entirely abolished under my plan. This is confirmed by the ready reckoners, on an accruals basis, each 1p cut in the starting rate reduces income by £590m; abolishing the tax altogether would suggest a static revenue loss of £5.9bn. The abolition of the starting rate will save money for every income tax payer in the country.

- ## Personal allowance

At the moment, people pay income tax and national insurance contributions at very low annual incomes. This means that already low wages are cut further; the result is that benefits and handouts are much higher than they need to be to obtain a given level of income post tax and benefits.

The simplest way of tackling this and reducing this 'churn' whereby people pay tax from one pocket and are given benefits into the other – and at the same time of reducing the welfare dependency trap – is to increase the personal allowance, for both income tax and national insurance contributions.

In 2005-06, the first £4,895 is free of tax (the personal allowance), with a higher personal allowance of £7,090 for people aged 65-74 and £7,220 for people aged 75 and over. However, there is also an aged person's limit of £19,500. If the total income, less allowable deductions of a taxpayer aged 65 or over exceeds this limit, the age-related allowances are reduced by £1 for each £2 of income over the aged income limit until the basic levels of the personal and married couple's allowances (MCA) are reached.

There is also a married couple's allowance of £5,905 for people born before 6 April 1935, rising to £5,975 for 75 and over. Blind people are eligible for an allowance of £1,610. After the allowances, the subsequent £2,090 of income is taxed at 10%; the

234 HMRC, Table 2.6, op. cit.

next £32,400 at 22% and the rest at 40%. In addition, men under the age of 65 and women under the age of 60 pay national insurance contributions.

Under my plan, there would be a personal allowance of £9,000 for everybody; even the oldest pensioners wouldn't lose out. But a personal allowance of £9,000 would reduce government revenues significantly on a static basis. An increase in the personal allowance by £100 reduces revenues by £620m on a static basis, the ready reckoners say. To avoid double counting and the effect of the abolition of the starting rate, increasing it from £6,985 (the original personal allowance plus the 10% tax band) to £9,000 would therefore represent a rise of £2015; the total value of the tax cut from the higher personal allowance would be £12.5bn.

- ## Closing loopholes

Under the present tax system, certain groups of taxpayers enjoy lower taxes if they behave in certain ways or invest their savings in special schemes (such as individual savings accounts). But under a flat tax, all these "reliefs" from regular tax rates (as the Treasury calls them) would be swept away. The Treasury lists all the main reliefs in a table in its ready reckoner (it is reproduced here as figure 21). In an unfortunate display of Treasury's tendency to assume that UK GDP belongs to the Chancellor, the document dubs the main tax reliefs "tax expenditures", suggesting that tax cuts or loopholes are a "cost" to the Treasury.

Because of the reductions in the top rate of tax and changes to the taxation of dividends, interest and investment income under the flat tax plan, it would not be possible simply to add all the loopholes together and to claim the entire value of the reliefs as extra revenue for the Treasury. Only part should count. The main reliefs listed in the Treasury's ready reckoners are reproduced in Figure 21.

FIGURE 21: PRINCIPAL TAX EXPENDITURES AND STRUCTURAL RELIEFS

Tax Expenditures	£ Million 2004-2005
Income Tax	
Relief for:	
Approved pension schemes	12,900
Share Incentive Plan	180
Approved savings-related share option	160
Enterprise Management Incentives	60
Personal Equity Plans	425
Individual Savings Accounts	1,200
Venture Capital Trusts	75
Enterprise Investment Scheme	180
Professional subscriptions	70
Rent a room	90
Exemption of:	
First £30,000 of payments on termination of employment	800
Interest on National Savings Certificates including index-linked certificates	120
Tax Exempt Special Savings Account interest	0
Premium Bond prizes	150
Income of charities	950
Foreign service allowed paid to Crown servants abroad	90
First £8,000 of reimbursted relocation packages provided by employers	300
Tax credits:	
Life assurance premiums (for contract made prior to 14 March 1984)	50
Child Tax Credit	3,000
Working Tax Credit	900
Corporation tax	
R&D tax credits	450
Relief for cleaning contaminated land	80
Income tax and corporation tax	
Film tax relief	70
National insurance contributions	
Relief for:	
Share Incentive Plan	120
Approved savings-related share option schemes	120
Employer contributions to approved pension schemes	6,600

Source: HM Treasury [235]

The analysis in this section is restricted to those reliefs relevant to income tax and excludes tax credits. I estimate that three-quarters of the relief for approved pensions would be recouped, or £8.55bn; the rest would not be because of the cuts to upper rate of tax. With some extra revenues generated by the abolition of some other loopholes, such as the ending of the "rent-a-room" loophole this might reach £9bn.

Static income tax cuts under the scheme would therefore be about £5.9bn for the starting rate, £13.7bn for the top rate, £12.5bn for the extra personal allowance,

---

235 HM Treasury, Tax Ready Reckoners, op. cit.

minus £9bn in tax hikes from the abolition of loopholes, which sums to a net £23.1bn for income tax alone.

National Insurance contributions

The current system

National Insurance contributions (NICs) differ very little in practice from income tax and have the same damaging effect on incentives.[236] The only – but highly significant – difference is the tax base: NICs only hit wages and income from self-employment (not other forms of income such as pensions or dividends); and it only affects women aged between 16 and 60 and men aged between 16 and 65. People of pensionable age who still work are exempt from NICs and only pay income tax. This crucial distinction is the main hurdle that makes it impossible to move immediately to a completely flat rate of tax in the UK; under my plan, as a temporary measure, pensioners would pay a lower rate of tax than the rest of the population. Pensioners would pay a flat rate of tax of 22% above the personal allowance; non-pensioners would pay 28%.

The UK Treasury maintains an elaborate accounting charade to back-up its pretence that NICs are different from income tax and used to finance a separate, independent social welfare system – in other words, that NICs are similar to insurance premiums.

In theory at least, the payment of NICs still entitles individuals to certain "contributory" social security benefits. These include the state pension. Contributions are paid into a so-called National Insurance Fund; a small, fixed proportion of this is allocated to the National Health Service and the remainder is used to finance contributory benefits.

In practice, however, as the Institute for Fiscal Studies points out, "contributions paid and benefits received bear little relation to each other for any individual contributor, and the link has weakened over time…The NI Fund is not a true fund in the sense that it has no significant balance available for investment: current contributions finance current benefits, with the fund merely being a device to prevent cash-flow problems."[237]

Officially, the value of the fund should not fall below one-sixth of national insurance expenditure, to ensure there is enough money available to pay benefits. In the past, a so-called 'grant' from central taxation has at times been required to make sure that this was possible, hence making a mockery of the whole system; however, the fund is currently in surplus.

---

236 For a complete analysis of NICs see: Government Actuary's Department, Report by the Government actuary of the drafts of the social security benefits up-rating order 2005 and the social security (contributions) (rerating and national insurance funds payments), Order 2005, February 2005, http://www.gad.gov.uk/Publications/docs/CM6457.pdf
237 'A Survey of the UK Tax System', Stuart Adam, *Institute for Fiscal Studies*, November 2004; http://www.ifs.org.uk/bns/bn09.pdf

As the Lib Dems put it: "A major source of complication is the separate National Insurance Contributions system. Although this now effectively starts at the same level of income as income tax, it is levied on a different definition of income (earnings only), on a weekly rather than annual basis, has an upper threshold for the 11% rate but not the 1% added in 2003, and also treats the self-employed differently. There is no longer any meaningful hypothecation of National Insurance which was the original justification for the separate system".

There is a clear and very strong case for abolishing the pretence that NICs are somehow separate from the rest of the tax code. The last formal link between contributions and benefits should be abolished, the non-existent trust fund relegated to the history books and the rest of the system swept away. Instead, NICs should be merged with the rest of income tax.

In a graphic illustration of the complexity of the modern UK tax system, NICs are divided into several classes.

Class 1 contributions are paid for by employees as a tax on their earnings (primary contributions) and employers as a wage tax on those they employ (secondary contributions).

Employee and employer NIC rates were both hiked by one percentage point in April 2003 by Brown to help pay for his public spending binge. Employees now have to pay NIC s at 11% on earnings between the Primary Threshold (£94 per week or £408 a month in 2005–06; equivalent to £4,896 a year, irritatingly one pound more than the income tax starting threshold) and the Upper Earnings Limit (£630 per week in 2005–06, an annualised £32,850), and at 1% on earnings above the Upper Earnings Limit. Employers pay NICs for each employee who earns over the Secondary Threshold (also set at £94 per week in 2005-06 or £408 a month, equivalent to £4,896 a year using the monthly figures), at a rate of 12.8% on all earnings above this level.

As the Institute for Fiscal Studies reminds us in its survey of the UK tax system, NICs are lower for those who have contracted out of the State Second Pension (formerly the State Earnings-Related Pension Scheme, SERPS) and have joined a private pension scheme. The tax cut depends on the type of scheme. For defined benefit pensions, the tax levied on earnings between the Primary Threshold/Secondary Threshold and the Upper Earnings Limit is reduced by 1.6 points for employee contributions and by 3.5 points for employer contributions. The equivalent rebates for those who have opted out into a defined contribution pension scheme depend on age.

The self-employed pay Class 2 and Class 4 NICs. Class 2 contributions are £2.10 a week for 2005–06 for people making more than £4,345 per year. Class 4 are an 8% tax on profits between the lower profits limit (£4.895 per year) and the upper profits limit (£32,760 per year), and at 1% on profits above that. The self-employed are therefore better off than the employed.

The most bizarre NIC is what must be Britain's only voluntary tax: Class 3 are voluntary and are usually made by UK citizens living abroad who wish to be entitled to benefits if they come back to the UK. Class 3 contributions are £7.35 per week for 2005-06.

The total net yield from national insurance contributions in 2005-06 is expected to be £85.9bn. Of that, a gross £36.821bn will come from Class 1(1) primary contributions, reduced to £34.440bn by contracting out of £2.380bn. Class 1(1) secondary contributions are expected to yield £52.311bn gross, reduced to a net £47.415bn by contracting out of £4.896bn. The total net Class 1(1) is therefore £81.855bn. Class 1A and B will bring in £968m, Class 2 will yield £282m, Class 3(3) will yield £89m, and Class 4 will yield £2.698bn.[238]

FIGURE 22: BRITAIN'S NATIONAL INSURANCE SYSTEM

			2005-06 (£m)
Class 1 (1)	Primary	Gross	36,821
		Contracted-out rebate (2)	2,380
		Net	34,440
	Secondary	Gross	52,311
		Contracted-out rebate (2)	4,896
		Net	47,415
	Total	Gross	89,132
		Contracted-out rebate (2)	7,277
		Net	81,855
Class 1A and 1B			968
Class 2			282
Class 3 (3)			89
Class 4			2,698
Total contributions			85,893

Source: Report by the Government actuary on the drafts of the social security benefits up-rating order 2005 and the Social Security (contributions) (rebating and National Insurance funds payments) Order 2005, February 2005, Cm 6457 [239]

Merging National Insurance contributions with income tax

Each of the following sections and bullet points describes a step in the proposed transformation and reduction of NICs and the effect of these changes on revenues. The end result would be to merge the transformed and much reduced employee NICs with (an equally reformed and reduced) income tax to produce a new flat tax on personal

---

238 Government Actuary's Department, op. cit.
239 Government Actuary's Department, op. cit.

income of 28% (with a special 22% rate for pensioners). All the official figures for government NIC receipts are those reproduced in Table 22.

Class 1(1) primary

- The first thing to do is to increase the starting threshold to align it to the new personal allowance of £9,000.
- According to HM Treasury, increasing the employee entry threshold by £2 per week would cut revenues by £245m. So taking the weekly limit from £94 to £173 (equivalent to £9,000 a year) is equivalent to boosting the limit by £79, or 39.5 times the £2 move suggested by the Treasury, would cut revenues by £9.67bn.
- This change would cut the revenue from Class 1(1) from a net £34.440bn to around £24.77bn
- Cutting what is left of Class 1(1) from 11% to 6% would cut the yield in a static manner to £13.5bn.
- However, this calculation would not include the entire effect of abolishing the top rate, which the Treasury estimates at £770m. To avoid double-counting, we assume this cuts revenues by an additional £400m to £13.1bn.
- Abolishing contracting out is assumed to bring in half its original amount of £2.38bn or around £1.2bn, taking the static revenue from what is left of Class 1(1) primary contributions to £14.3bn
- Finally, the Upper Earnings Limit needs to be increased from £32,850 to £37,295 to align this with the top rate of tax. A guess is that this would take the combined yield of what is left of Class 1(1) primary NICs back up by £1.3bn a year, increasing the total yield to the Treasury to £15.6bn
- The overall result of the reforms described would be to reduce class 1(1) primary NIC revenue by about £18.8bn on a static basis to £15.6bn, down from £34.44bn.

Class 1(1) secondary

- The first step is to abolish contracting out for pensions, boosting revenues by £4.896bn from employers.[240]
- NIC relief for savings-related share option schemes (which according to the Treasury is equivalent of tax cut of £110m a year) and the share incentive plan (worth £110m a year to taxpayers) would also both be abolished. The total tax increase would be £5.1bn.

---

240 The figures, from the Government Actuary's Department, op. cit., are actually lower than those in the Treasury ready reckoners, which predicts £5.8bn for this year

- For the time being, Class 1(1) secondary NICs would remain at 12.8%; employers will be compensated by cuts in corporation tax (see below).

Class 1A and 1B

- These are charged at 12.8% and are set to yield £1bn. Class 1A is a tax on benefits in kind paid for by employers; Class 1B deals with sundry benefits
- These two taxes would be left unchanged for the time being.

Class 2

- These would be abolished, cutting static revenues by £282m a year.

Class 3

- These would be abolished, cutting static revenues by £89m a year.

Class 4

NICs for the self-employed would be merged into income tax, in the same way as for employees. The starting threshold (or lower profits limit) would be raised to £9,000 from £4,895; and the 8% rate be cut to 6%, which means that there will no longer be any advantages to being self-employed. The additional 1% rate would also be abolished to ensure a maximum top overall tax rate of 28%. NICs will have to paid up to £37,295 to align this with the top rate of tax.

According to the ready reckoners, changing the lower profit limit by £104 a year cuts revenues by £20m; so the total static revenue reduction would be around £790m a year. The revenue loss from scrapping the additional 1% rate would be £185m. Cutting the main rate by one percentage point would cut revenues by £335m, according to the ready reckoners; so taking the 8% rate to 6% would reduce revenues on a static basis by £670m. The NIC extension may raise another £200m. The total revenue loss from Class 4 cuts would therefore be £1.445bn.

The total net static revenue loss from these reforms to National Insurance contributions would be £17bn. Under the reform, the top rate is abolished; the marginal rate cut from 11% to 6%; the starting rate aligned with income tax; and the personal allowance for both income tax and NIC set at £9,000. The result would be a 0% tax on the first £9,000 earned and then 28% on the rest. While still much too high, it would nevertheless represent a massive 13-point cut in the top tax rate.

Corporation tax

Corporation tax has a starting rate of 0%, a small companies' rate of 19% and a main rate of 30%. The system is complicated. The starting rate is for companies making less than £10,000 a year; companies earning between £10,000 and £50,000 pay 23.75% on that tranche of profits; the small companies' rate applies to profits below £300,000; profits between £300,000 and £1.5m are taxed at 32.75%; and profits above £1.5m are taxed at 30%. Brown announced at his December 2005 Pre-Budget Report that the 0% rate would go and former beneficiaries would also pay 19% tax.

The first step is to sweep all exemptions to this away. Schemes that would be scrapped include R&D tax credits that the Treasury estimates is equivalent to a £430m tax cut, relief for clearing contaminated land worth £75m, film tax relief worth £140m, a share incentive plan worth £110m, approved savings-related share option schemes worth £110m (employer contributions to approved pension schemes would also be abolished, as pointed out earlier) . The total comes to around £865m in targeted tax cuts which would all be repealed to allow for a lower overall flat tax rate.

A simple (but not entirely satisfactory) reform would be to make profits between 0 and £300,000 a year completely tax free and then impose a 28% on all profits above that level. The Treasury ready reckoner says that to change the small companies' rate by 1 percentage point would change yield by £180m. This implies that abolishing it completely would cut revenues on a static basis by £3.4bn. Cutting corporation tax by 1 percentage point would cut revenue by about £1bn a year for 2005-06, according to the Treasury; so the total would come to £5.4bn under this option. From this £865m should be subtracted, taking the next tax cuts to £4.535bn.

This is not ideal: the new 28% tax rate would be accompanied by other taxes on business, including employers NICs and business rates; and under Hall-Rabushka, all corporate income should be taxed, with no allowance.

Personal Savings

Savings income is taxed at 10% up to the starting rate limit, at 20% between the starting and basic rate limits and 40% above. In 2005-06, taxes on savings are expected to bring in £140m from starting rate taxpayers, £2,080 from basic rate taxpayers and £1,790 from top rate taxpayers, a total of £4.01bn.[241] These should all be abolished. Together with the changes to dividends tax and capital gains tax, it would become much easier to save: there would no longer be any need for tax advice or vehicles such as Individual Savings Accounts (ISAs).

---

241 HMRC, Table 2.6, Income tax liabilities, by taxpayer's marginal rate, 2005-06, op. cit

Dividends

Dividends are currently liable for income tax at 10% up to the basic rate limit and 32.5% above; however, for those taxpayers who are eligible, a 10% tax credit reduces the liability. According to HMRC, top-rate taxpayers will pay £4.9bn in income tax on dividends in 2005-06 and basic rate taxpayers £1.3bn, totaling £6.2bn.[242]

One of the flat tax's most dramatic contributions would therefore be to boost the value of shares: assuming a price to earnings ratio of just 15 times, boosting the revenues from equities by around £6.2bn a year could be expected to increase share prices by £93bn. The abolition of the tax on dividends would align the UK with Slovakia, where making dividends tax free has worked very well.

In the short term, HMRC would probably have to stipulate that shareholder/owners of small and other businesses continue paying themselves a market wage. This would be to prevent them from working for free and paying themselves entirely in dividends – and thus paying no tax at all under this proposal.

Capital Gains Tax

At the moment, Capital Gains Tax rules are fiendishly complex, with at last count 39 potential effective tax rates depending on asset type, how long it has been owned for and in what context. The top rate is 40% for non-business assets and can be as low as 24% for assets held 10 years or more; for business assets, the range is 40% to 10%, calculated according to a complex taper system.

Capital Gains Tax yielded a mere £2.32bn in 2003-04[243]; for 2005-06 the prediction is for £3bn, according to the Budget.[244]

The official justification for Capital Gains Tax is that it is necessary to prevent a massive haemorrhage of government revenues. According to the IFS, "capital gains tax is potentially important as an anti-avoidance measure, as it discourages wealthier individuals from converting a large part of their income into capital gains in order to reduce their tax liability".[245]

Like the abolition of the tax on dividends, this would need clever monitoring to prevent too great a loss in tax revenues. Some have argued that it would be necessary to continue taxing capital gains as regular income for assets retained for less than two years and to make it tax free after that to avoid too many people converting their income into capital gains for tax purposes;[246] this would not be my favourite option and should only be used as a back-up if no other solution is found.

---

242 HMRC, Table 2.6, Income tax liabilities, by taxpayer's marginal rate, 2005-06, op. cit
243 HMRC, Table 14.2, Capital Gains Tax, 2003-04, http://www.hmrc.gov.uk/stats/capital_gains/14_2_sep05.pdf
244 Budget 2005, HM Treasury, p250; http://www.hm-treasury.gov.uk/media/B5B/80/bud05_completereport_147.pdf
245 IFS, UK tax system, op. cit
246 John Redwood (2004), *Singing the Blues: The Once and Future Conservatives*, Politico's Publishing

Inheritance Tax

Inheritance tax is expected to yield £3.4bn in 2005-06[247]. As Hall-Rabushka argued, it is a form of double-taxation and should therefore be abolished. The dynamic effects from the move would be the savings in terms of accounting costs and other tax-dodging costs; but it would also turn the UK into a tax haven for rich, older people and their families. Many would move to Britain, taking their assets with them. They would also spend more in the UK, boosting VAT revenues, and buy houses and property. The abolition of inheritance tax would align the UK with countries such as Estonia.

Total tax cuts

The total gross tax cuts proposed are worth £77.4bn and the tax increases (through the abolition of loopholes and alignment of NICs Upper Earnings Limit with the start of the upper rate of income tax) worth £17.7bn. So the net tax cut would be £59.7bn on a static basis, before dynamic and other effects kick in. This is around 5% of GDP. I have not included any estimate for reduced tax credits in these numbers.

FIGURE 23: TOTAL TAX CUTS IN HEATH FLAT TAX

Tax	(Cuts)	Increases	Net
Income tax	(£32.1bn)	£9bn	(£23.1bn)
Employee National Insurance Contributions	(£23.3bn)	£2.7bn	(£20.6bn)
Employer National Insurance Contributions	0	£5.1bn	£5.1bn
Corporation Tax	(£5.4bn)	£865m	(£4.5bn)
Savings Tax	(£4bn)	0	(£4bn)
Dividend Tax	(£6.2bn)	0	(£6.2bn)
Capital Gains Tax	(£3bn)	0	(£3bn)
Inheritance Tax	(£3.4bn)	0	(£3.4bn)
Total	(£77.4bn)	£17.7bn	(£59.7bn)

Dynamic effects

A conservative estimate of the Laffer-type, growth and reduced avoidance effects of a flat tax is to assume that around 40% of the cuts to income tax, national insurance contributions and corporation tax would be made up in extra revenues over a period of three years.

Less realistically, no feedback effect will be assumed from the abolition of the

---

247 Budget 2005, p250

146

tax on dividends, capital gains, inheritance and investment income. In practice, given that the UK would immediately attract huge amounts of investment from overseas and some of this money would spill over into taxable income, this is undoubtedly far too pessimistic an assumption. These ultra-minimal feedback effects are expected to reduce the tax cut by £17.2bn a year after three years.

Restraining public spending

Total managed expenditure is expected to reach £518.6bn in 2005-06, rising to £549.2bn in 2006-07 and £580bn in 2007-08. After that, as explained in the 2005 Budget, the Treasury assumes that public sector current expenditure in 2008-09 will grow by 1.9% in real terms, in line with the assumed growth rate in the 2004 Pre-Budget Report, and by the same rate of 1.9% in 2009-10.[248] If we assume that these growth rates are applicable to the whole of total managed expenditure and inflation of 2.5%, growth would therefore be 4.4% in cash terms in both years. This would take total spending to £605.5bn in 2008-09 and £632.2bn in 2009-10.

The easiest way to plug any revenue shortfall under a flat tax would be to freeze public expenditure in real terms, allowing spending to grow by just 2.5% a year in cash terms to keep up for inflation. This would mean that public spending would reach £531.5bn in 2006-07, £544.8bn in 2007-08, £558.4bn in 2008-09 and £572.4bn in 2009-2010.

So allowing public spending to rise by 2.5% a year in cash terms but no more over the first four years of the flat tax (assuming a 2006-07 start) would save a massive £59.8bn a year, by coincidence almost exactly the 2005-06 static value of the tax cuts. Of course, by then, the static revenue loss from the flat tax would have gone up from the original figure.

In the first year alone, spending restraints would save almost £18bn, cutting the amount needed to balance the books at £24bn. Because the savings are so great, after 3 years they may allow additional tax cuts; alternatively, keeping spending growth at 2.5% a year for 3 years might be enough (see figure 24).

Cutting waste

Restraining the growth of future public spending should also be accompanied by a program to cut unnecessary public spending. The Department for Trade and Industry should be abolished; HM Revenue & Customs has a budget of £4.6bn in 2005-06: a large chunk of this could be cut under a flat tax. Payments for the CAP are expected to be £3.3bn in 2005-06. If these were withheld, more money could be saved. There have been three separate reports on government waste. The Taxpayers' Alliance found £82bn in govern-

---

ment waste, the James Review identified nearly £35bn of administrative savings and the Gershon report identified administrative savings of £21.5bn by 2008, mainly to be delivered by cutting departmental budgets and moving civil servants out of London. The indications are that the Gershon savings are unlikely all to be introduced; but even in the extremely unlikely event that they were, there is much more fat left in the British government. The target should be to save £25bn a year after 2 years; as the figures in Figure 24 suggest even that may not be necessary.

Selling assets

Some additional revenue raising and saving measures would be necessary in the short term. A relatively straightforward way of doing this would be to accelerate the sell-off of state assets. Obvious targets should include BNFL, the Post Office, the assets of the Shareholder Executive and the government's huge land holdings. The aim ought to be to increase the disposal of government assets by at least £15bn immediately after the introduction of the flat tax.

Borrowing

An increase in the debt to GDP ratio over a period of five years, if accompanied by a rigorous program to sell the change to the financial markets, should be acceptable. Any objections from the EU should be dismissed out of hand as tax policy should never have become part of its remit. It is worth incurring some additional borrowing for the sake of moving to a dramatically more efficient tax system. In Figure 24, borrowing of only £9.3bn is needed in the first year; after that the savings and dynamic effects would soon allow for this extra debt and much more to be repaid.

FIGURE 24: PAYING FOR THE FLAT TAX

Revenue source	Year 1 (per year)	Year 2 (per year)	Year 3 (per year)
Dynamic feedback effect	£5.7bn	£11.4bn	£17.2bn
Spending restraint	£17.7bn	£35.2bn	£47.1bn
War on waste	£12bn	£25bn	£25bn
Privatisation	£15bn	0	0
Borrowing	£9.3bn	0	0
Total	£59.7bn	£71.6bn	£89.3bn

Notes: These figures are no more than schematic; the forecast for the dynamic feedback effect has deliberately been kept artificially low to ensure that these estimates remain conservative. For the sake of simplicity, the table also assumes that all values except for the public spending freeze are frozen in today's money. This is unrealistic but does not materially affect the overall conclusion.

Winners from the flat tax

The following table is based on much more detailed information than that presented previously. It looks at deciles, not just quintiles; and the definition of income used is original income (i.e. before benefits in cash and in kind, this is a different definition from that used in figure 12).

FIGURE 25: A STATIC ANALYSIS OF THE HEATH FLAT TAX [249]

Decile Groups											
Average per household (£ per year)	Bottom (£)	2nd (£)	3rd (£)	4th (£)	5th (£)	6th (£)	7th (£)	8th (£)	9th (£)	Top (£)	All Households
Wages and salaries	1,340	3,110	5,382	9,368	13,884	18,617	22,556	29,741	36,014	58,843	19,885
Imputed income from benefits in kind	8	0	26	30	97	144	278	432	716	1,573	330
Self-employment income	439	578	695	1,268	1,018	1,346	2,232	2,522	4,326	12,745	2,717
Occupational pensions, annuities	401	890	1,250	1,871	2,216	2,623	2,520	3,021	2,962	3,515	2,127
Investment income	256	233	240	381	480	563	612	917	1,452	3,572	871
Other income	141	99	113	187	219	221	269	161	226	360	200
Total income from work, occupational pensions, investments and private sources	2,586	4,910	7,706	13,105	17,915	23,514	28,467	36,794	45,695	80,608	26,130
Income Tax	287	455	854	1,548	2,258	3,170	4,190	5,675	7,478	16,287	4,220
Tax credits	-16	-96	-170	-271	-232	-211	-186	-167	-65	-21	-144
Employee National Insurance Contributions	92	183	330	610	925	1,301	1,622	2,161	2,616	3,326	1,317
IT + ENIC	379	638	1,184	2,158	3,183	4,471	5,812	7,836	10,094	19,613	5,537
Flat Tax Taxable income[250]	0	0	0	3,724	8,435	13,951	18,855	26,877	35,243	68,036	16,259
Flat tax	0	0	0	1,043	2,361	3,906	5,279	7,525	9,868	19,050	4,552
Income boost	379	638	1,184	1,115	822	565	533	311	226	563	985
Boost, %	14.7%	13%	15.3%	8.5%	4.6%	2.4%	1.8%	0.8%	0.5%	0.7%	3.8%
Current IT + ENIC tax rate, %	14.7%	13%	15.3%	16.5%	17.7%	19%	20.3%	21.2%	22.1%	24.3%	21.2%
Flat tax rate, %	0%	0%	0%	7.9%	13.2%	16.6%	18.5%	20.4%	21.6%	23.6%	17.4%

The results are remarkable. Under a 28% flat tax (with merged income tax and National

---

249 Original data sourced from Office for National Statistics, Table 14, Appendix 1, http://www.statistics.gov.uk/STATBASE/Expodata/Spreadsheets/D8228.xls

250 Assumptions:
* one-earner households so only one personal allowance; this under-estimates the real size of the tax cuts given the huge rise in the personal allowance under the proposed flat tax
* £9,000 or below, 0% tax
* £9,000 or above, 28% on all income except investment income
* Investment income, 0% tax
* This exaggerates the amount of tax paid by pensioner households, who would pay only 22% on wages and self-employment income

Insurance contributions), a £9,000 personal allowance and the assumption of no taxes on investment income:

- at least 8m households would pay no direct tax on their income at all the poorest three and a bit deciles would see their original income (excluding indirect taxes and benefits) surge by between 13-15%; the reform would be tantamount to a pay rise of the same amount and would boost the incentives of those on lower incomes to work and get off benefits
- the top three deciles would enjoy an income boost of just 0.5% to 0.8%. Even in cash terms, the second lowest decile would enjoy a boost of that is considerably greater (at £638) than that of the top three deciles (they would gain only by £226 to £563).
- the direct system would remain progressive, with the first three deciles paying no tax and the next seven paying a progressively higher tax rate

Future reforms

Other important reforms should be introduced – though they need not necessarily take place at the same time as the others. Following the model set out in Hall-Rabushka, Britain should move towards the immediate expensing of all capital spending for corporation tax purposes; this would be equivalent to making all depreciation instantaneous for tax. In 2002-03, the latest year for which data was available, the total value of capital allowances reported was £72.301bn, according to HMRC.[251] These had the effect of reducing gross trading profit from £194.5bn to £139.5bn. The figures for capital allowances are the amounts which companies claim in the period, less balancing charges. If capital allowances exceed the gross trading profit, leading to a loss for tax purposes, net trading profits fall to zero – there are no negative figures. Losses brought forward are not deducted in arriving at net trading profits.

At the same time as immediately expensing all capital spending, interest payments should cease to be tax-deductible on all new debt; to ensure that companies in the aggregate do not lose out, national insurance contributions for employers should be cut by exactly the same amount.

A tax form on a postcard

Following these reforms, the aim would be for tax forms to be limited to just two. The first would represent most personal income and would cover salaries paid today under pay as you earn (PAYE); the second, for business income, would also cover the work of freelancers and the self-employed. The first tax form could easily be filled in by

---

251 Corporation tax computation of liability 2002-03, HMRC, Table 11.5, http://www.hmrc.gov.uk/stats/corporate_tax/11_4_oct05.pdf

employers, whose overall burden would be much reduced by these reforms. The second would be filled in by businesses, the self-employed and those earning additional income not covered under pay-as-you-earn.

A growth and asset price boom

The reduction in deadweight loss from this flat tax proposal would be huge. But it is impossible to be sure by how much economic growth would be boosted by the introduction in the UK of a comprehensive Hall-Rabushka-style flat tax, accompanied by a significant reduction in the public spending to GDP ratio. There are no full models of the UK economy available to gauge what would happen to the supply of labour and capital under such a reform.

However, it is a fair guess from the academic literature that a flat tax combined with a significant reduction in the share of tax in GDP would boost economic growth in the UK by at least 0.5 percentage points a year.[252] The flat tax reforms would have to be accompanied by continued liberal migration policies, a vigorous commitment to low inflation from an independent Bank of England and a freeing up of restraints on house and commercial property building to allow the supply of labour, homes and offices to keep up.

Meanwhile, without any remedial action and the continued accumulation of red tape and higher taxes, the UK economy's trend (long-term sustainable) rate of growth will fall over the next 10 years: instead of today's 2.5% (or 2.75%, depending on estimates), it is likely to decline to closer to 2.25% or even 2%. So even a 1% increase in growth should not be seen as an overly optimistic estimate from the reforms outlined in this book.

Even small increases in growth can make a huge difference. If instead of growing by (say) 2% a year, the economy were to grow by 2.5% a year, the long-term boost to growth would be immense. Over a period of 10 years, taking the 2004 figure of real GDP of £1.16 trillion, the UK economy would grow by 21.9% under the current policy scenario to £1.4104 trillion; under a flat tax, it would grow by 28.01% to £1.4849 trillion. The difference is worth £74.5bn a year after a decade: it is equivalent to saying that every one of Britain's 24.7m households would be £3,016 a year better off thanks to a flat tax.

The value of their assets would also increase much faster under a flat tax. Wages, share prices and house prices arguably tend to grow in line with nominal GDP. Assuming inflation of 2.5% over the long term and real economic growth going up from 2% to 2.5%, a flat tax would see wages, share prices and house prices grow by 5% a year instead of 4.5% a year, an 11.1% increase in their rate of growth.

---

252 Leach, op. cit., calculates that "government policy will reduce long-term GDP growth in the UK by 0.3% to 0.5% per annum. Trend growth will decline towards 2% per annum". At the same time, he thinks cutting the tax to GDP ratio to around 30% would boost growth to 3%. A flat tax could have an even greater impact.

Chapter X: Conclusion

As David Blunkett's biographer Stephen Pollard puts it in a recent pamphlet on the future of British politics, "Advocacy of a flat tax presses all the right buttons. It is good for the economy. It is good for the poor. It is good for business. And it is easy to grasp."[253]

The results of the simulation for my 28% flat tax plan with merged NICs and income tax, zero double taxation of profits and a £9,000 personal allowance show that the poor would benefit hugely from a flat tax; the rich would at first gain almost nothing on average because of the elimination of their favourite loopholes but the massively lower marginal tax rates they would face would still lead to an explosion of work, risk-taking and entrepreneurship, giving the economy a huge fillip. We have also seen that a combination of feedback effects, limiting public spending growth to 2.5% a year in cash terms, abolishing a few unnecessary spending programs such as corporate welfare or the Department of Trade and Industry would go most or all of the way towards filling the static tax cut of £60bn this would represent. An accelerated privatisation program could plug any temporary shortfall; if required, the government could borrow a little more. For a Chancellor who has borrowed well over £100bn more than originally forecast barely 5 years ago, a few more billion would make little difference. The Treasury always talks about it being fine to borrow "to invest" in capital spending projects (which are in fact often of dubious value); there is equally nothing wrong in "investing" in a much more efficient tax system and faster economic growth over the long run by borrowing a few billion pounds to ease any transition to a flat tax.

However, the first lesson of the Christian Democrats' miserable performance in the German elections – apart from the need for competent leadership and campaigning – is that in the current climate of opinion radical ideas – such as a flat tax or even radical tax cuts that fall short of a truly flat system – need to be argued for, explained and propagated for many years before an election. Campaign groups that mobilise and educate grass roots activists are especially important to any successful campaign for lower taxes, as demonstrated time and again in the US.

The second mistake made by Merkel was her insistence that a huge hike to value added tax accompany any reduction in payroll taxes. Her mindset was clearly static and hence deeply flawed. Huge tax hikes that would hit the poor especially badly, combined with cuts to an invisible tax paid by employers and vague talk of a flat tax and the abolition of the top rate of income tax: that was no recipe for electoral success. It would be a terrible mistake for the British political elite and commentariat to dismiss the flat tax as a result of Merkel's poor performance – as well as a gross misunderstanding of the real lessons of the German election.

Much more important would be the Brown Treasury's reaction to any serious proposal by opposition parties to introduce a flat tax in the UK. In a recent article in

253 Stephen Pollard (2005), *From Labour To... ?*, Centre for Policy Studies, London, 2005: http://www.cps.org.uk/pdf/pub/414.pdf

The Guardian, its economics editor, Larry Elliott, cogently argued that there are three arguments which Brown will deploy to try and destroy any flat tax proposal.[254] First, he would ask the Tories for a breakdown of the anticipated winners and losers from a flat tax and would use figures such as those calculated by Lombard Street Research to claim that most people (bar the very wealthy) would lose and to claim that the Tories only care about the rich. My response to this is that any political party that endorses a flat tax should reject these findings out of hand and present instead a plan for a flat tax calculated to ensure that virtually everybody pays less tax, especially the poor. My plan shows that the poor would gain much more in a static analysis than the rich; and that the top deciles would see almost no difference at all. The kind of numbers presented in this paper would destroy Brown's first argument. Of course, the flat tax plan would have to be accompanied by a significant reduction in the rate of growth of public spending and the other changes described above.

Larry Elliott's next point is that if it were to be suggested that the flat tax could be made progressive by raising personal allowances, Brown would ask the Tories which bits of public spending they intended to cut as a result of falling tax revenues. "The idea that greater incentives will make good £63bn of lost tax revenues will be one heck of a tricky political sell", he says. Again, my response is that flat tax supporters should point to the available academic literature to argue that around 40% (or a similar figure) of the static revenue losses would be recouped through dynamic effect; they should present this proposition as not only empirically and theoretically rigorous but also obviously common sense. To help buttress their argument, they ought to launch a campaign to ensure that tax forecasting be conducted using dynamic assumptions and commission a major international economic consultancy or a team of academics to develop a dynamic model for the UK economy. This could then be used with devastating effect to counter attacks from the Treasury. To help smooth the transition, my plan also suggests that several useless items of spending should be abolished. In the run-up to the last election, Labour, the Tories and the Liberal Democrats all agreed to wage war on waste; even though Brown will (wrongly) claim that his efficiency drive is proceeding successfully and that no more fat remains to be cut, the public will not be convinced. In addition to keeping state spending growth to the rate of inflation, supporters of the flat tax should therefore launch a campaign to cut significant amounts of wasteful or useless spending a year. This should include the Department of Trade and Industry, handouts to farmers through the EU as well as much else besides. No frontline services in health, education or the police should be cut.

Brown's final argument would be that the hidden agenda for the flat tax crowd is to shrink the size of the state and make individuals pay their own way when it comes to education and health. The response should be that yes, part of the reason for the flat tax is to reduce the size of the state, which has grown horrendously bloated. However, it

---

254 'Flat tax does not mean a level playing field', Larry Elliott, October 10, 2005, *The Guardian*,
http://politics.guardian.co.uk/economics/comment/0,11268,1588671,00.htm

remains possible to retain a smaller state and keep health and education public, as they currently are, if that is what is desired by mainstream opinion in the UK. The issue of reducing the size of the state and privatising health and education are two different ones; they should not be confused in the context of arguing for the flat tax. The public is extraordinarily concerned about waste in the public sector; it should not be very difficult for a clear-headed and professional campaign to convince people that this is the salient issue, rather than any plan to make people pay to attend state schools.

It is true that the original euphoria about introducing a flat tax in the UK is gone. But when the cold light of day is shined on the proposal, as this book has done, the conclusions are nevertheless clear:

- A flat tax is an immensely desirable medium-term aim for the UK.
- No country has yet adopted a full, comprehensive flat tax, though some Eastern European countries have successfully come close.
- It will not be possible to move immediately to a full flat tax in the UK. The British state is too big and the tax system too complex. A key problem is the existence of national insurance contributions on employers and the fact that pension income and income from employment for pensioners is free from NICs and hence taxed at a lower rate than other income.
- Nevertheless, a radical overhaul of the UK tax system which went much of the way towards a flat tax could quickly be implemented; over time a full flat tax would become possible.
- The British tax reform debate must be about more than merely fiddling with income tax, abolishing a couple of exemptions or slightly increasing the personal allowance. The discussion should focus on including National Insurance contributions in a new, broader tax on income; it should examine taxes on capital and interest, abolish the double taxation of profits and simplify corporation tax.
- Whereas employees' national insurance contributions should be merged with income tax, employers' contribution should continue for the time being and eventually abolished. Most people don't realise they exist.
- A flat tax system whereby very few people – if anyone – ends up paying more tax can be designed – the one suggested in this book is one possible version.
- However, such a system entails significantly lower public spending as a share of GDP in the future than currently planned by Brown. A flat tax with minimal losers can only be successfully introduced in the UK if, over time, the size of the state is reduced significantly. This policy, which would be desirable in itself, will require a cultural shift in the UK policy debate. Crucially, while opponents such as Brown will claim that this is equivalent to calling for huge

spending cuts, this is not the case. A flat tax and a lower tax to GDP ratio can be achieved even if spending continues to go up, albeit by less than the rate of economic growth, as we have shown.

- The process would nevertheless be made easier if it were accompanied by other transitional measures, including a war on waste, the abolition of currently existing but wasteful and value destroying government programmes such as the Department of Trade and Industry.
- There may also be a need for temporary additional borrowing to help pay for the transition from the current failing tax system to a flat tax. Supporters of a flat tax should not be ashamed of this and should argue that this would represent a small "investment" that would repay itself many times over the next few years thanks to the additional growth, jobs, higher wages and increased capital values that it would generate.
- Any need for transitional borrowing could be reduced by an acceleration in the sell-off of state assets.
- Crucially, however, no plan for a flat tax is feasible without assuming positive feedback effects and that at least some of the tax cut will pay for itself. Unless the dynamic effects of a flat tax are acknowledged, and the vast empirical and theoretical literature which shows that a large share of the revenues 'lost' from the tax cuts will be recovered via greater effort, faster economic growth and reduced tax avoidance, is accepted, no progress will ever be made. Supporters of the flat tax who wrongly concede to their opponents that supply-side and dynamic effects should not be included in simulations of the effects of a flat tax or of a lower overall tax to GDP ratio are shooting themselves in the foot.
- It is crucial that supporters of a flat tax with a big personal allowance grab the moral high ground and paint a picture of a better, fairer society. All flat tax proposals must include huge tax cuts for the poor and those on lower than average incomes. My own proposals would benefit the poor far more than they would help the rich.

While the UK is procrastinating over the flat tax, it is becoming increasingly uncompetitive in the global market for capital and skilled workers, with even governments that have no truck with the radicalism of a fully flat tax nevertheless busily trimming marginal rates on income, profits, capital gains, dividends and inheritance. Over the next decade, the flat tax will be to politics and the global economy what privatisation was to the 1980s and 1990s: it will rejuvenate those countries that adopt it first, while relegating those that drag their feet to a second economic division characterised by sluggish growth, rising unemployment and reduced living standards. The race to be the first Western country with a flat tax is on; the rewards for the winner will be immense.